The Social Bases of Nazism, 1919–1933

This latest addition to *New Studies in Economic and Social History* sheds fascinating light on an essential aspect of the history of Nazism. The social background of the supporters of Nazism has been the subject of intense debate since the early 1930s. Was the Nazi Party a predominantly middle-class party or a people's party? Detlef Mühlberger provides a comprehensive summary of the answer to this question, based on extensive sociological and psephological evidence. The data support the claim made by the Nazis in the 1920s and early 1930s that their party was a *Volkspartei* able to mobilise support from all sections of German society. Lucidly written and clearly illustrated with numerous figures and tables, this book will be essential reading for all those interested in modern German history.

DETLEF MÜHLBERGER is a Lecturer in Modern European History at Oxford Brookes University. He has published widely on various aspects of Nazism; his books include *Hitler's Followers: Studies in the Sociology of the Nazi Movement* and *Hitler's Voice: The Völkischer Beobachter, 1920–1933*.

New Studies in Economic and Social History

Edited for the Economic History Society by
Maurice Kirby
Lancaster University

This series, specially commissioned by the Economic History Society, provides a guide to the current interpretations of the key themes of economic and social history in which advances have recently been made or in which there has been significant debate.

In recent times economic and social history has been one of the most flourishing areas of historical study. This has mirrored the increasing relevance of the economic and social sciences both in a student's choice of career and in forming a society at large more aware of the importance of these issues in their everyday lives. Moreover specialist interests in business, agricultural and welfare history, for example, have themselves burgeoned and there has been an increased interest in the economic development of the wider world. Stimulating as these scholarly developments have been for the specialist, the rapid advance of the subject and the quantity of new publications make it difficult for the reader to gain an overview of particular topics, let alone the whole field.

New Studies in Economic and Social History is intended for students and their teachers. It is designed to introduce them to fresh topics and to enable them to keep abreast of recent writing and debates. All the books in the series are written by a recognised authority in the subject, and the arguments and issues are set out in a critical but unpartisan fashion. The aim of the series is to survey the current state of scholarship, rather than to provide a set of prepackaged conclusions.

The series has been edited since its inception in 1968 by Professors M. W. Flinn, T. C. Smout and L. A. Clarkson, and is currently edited by Professor Maurice Kirby. From 1968 it was published by Macmillan as *Studies in Economic History,* and after 1974 as *Studies in Economic and Social History.* From 1995 *New Studies in Economic and Social History* is being published on behalf of the Economic History Society by Cambridge University Press. This new series includes some of the titles previously published by Macmillan as well as new titles, and reflects the ongoing development throughout the world of this rich seam of history.

For a full list of titles in print, please see the end of the book.

The Social Bases of Nazism, 1919–1933

Prepared for the Economic History Society by

Detlef Mühlberger
Oxford Brookes University

PUBLISHED BY THE PRESS SYNDICATE OF THE UNIVERSITY OF CAMBRIDGE
The Pitt Building, Trumpington Street, Cambridge CB2 1RP, United Kingdom

CAMBRIDGE UNIVERSITY PRESS
The Edinburgh Building, Cambridge, CB2 2RU, UK
40 West 20th Street, New York, NY 10011–4211, USA
477 Williamstown Road, Port Melbourne, VIC 3207, Australia
Ruiz de Alarcón 13, 28014 Madrid, Spain
Dock House, The Waterfront, Cape Town 8001, South Africa

http://www.cambridge.org

First published 2003

Printed in the United Kingdom at the University Press, Cambridge

Typeface Plantin 10/12.5 pt.   *System* LaTeX 2_ε [TB]

A catalogue record for this book is available from the British Library

Library of Congress cataloguing in publication data
Mühlberger, Detlef.
The social bases of Nazism, 1919–1933 / prepared for the Economic History Society
by D. Mühlberger.
    p.   cm. – (New studies in economic and social history; 48)
Includes bibliographical references and index.
ISBN 0 521 80285 7 – ISBN 0 521 00372 5 (pb.)
1. National socialism – Social aspects.   2. Nationalsozialistische Deutsche
Arbeiter-Partei.
I. Economic History Society.   II. Title.   III. Series.
DD256.5.M754   2003
324.243′038′09042–dc21   2003046057

ISBN 0 521 80285 7 hardback
ISBN 0 521 00372 5 paperback

Contents

Figures

Tables

Note on references

References in the text within square brackets relate to the numbered items in the Bibliography, followed, where necessary, by the page numbers in italics, for example [1: *1–10*].

Acknowledgements

I am indebted to Professors Jürgen Falter, Conan Fischer and Paul Madden for the helpful advice which they have given me over the years on the theme under review in this book. I would also like to thank Anne Lloyd and Matthew Feldman for their support and assistance. My thanks as well to Elizabeth Howard and Helen Barton for their helpful editorial advice. I am particularly grateful for the support and encouragement I have received while preparing this book from Professor Maurice Kirby.

Abbreviations

BDC	Berlin Document Center
BNSDJ	*Bund Nationalsozialistischer Deutscher Juristen* (League of National Socialist German Lawyers)
DAP	*Deutsche Arbeiterpartei* (German Workers' Party)
HJ	*Hitlerjugend* (Hitler Youth)
KPD	*Kommunistische Partei Deutschlands* (Communist Party of Germany)
NSBO	*Nationalsozialistische Betriebszellenorganisation* (National Socialist Factory Cell Organisation)
NSDÄB	*Nationalsozialistischer Deutscher Ärztebund* (National Socialist German Doctors' League)
NSDAP	*Nationalsozialistische Deutsche Arbeiterpartei* (National Socialist German Workers' Party or Nazi Party)
NSF	*Nationalsozialistische Frauenschaft* (National Socialist Women's League)
NSLB	*Nationalsozialistischer Lehrerbund* (National Socialist Teachers' League)
SA	*Sturmabteilung* (Storm Section)
SPD	*Sozialdemokratische Partei Deutschlands* (Social Democratic Party of Germany)
SS	*Schutzstaffel* (Protection Squad)
SS–TV	*SS–Totenkopfverbände* (SS–Death's Head Formations)
SS–VT	*SS–Verfügungstruppe* (SS–Specialist Troops)

Chapter 1

Introduction

The question under consideration in this study is 'Who were the Nazis?', the answer to which is critical to our understanding of the Nazi phenomenon. For the historian and social scientist, discovering the nature of Nazi support is obviously not an esoteric exercise, for it is only by identifying as precisely as possible *those who were Nazis* that a meaningful answer can be given to another fundamental question, namely *why individuals joined the Nazi Party* in their hundreds of thousands before 30 January 1933, the day on which Hitler was appointed chancellor of the Weimar Republic. The main concern here will be to investigate the support mobilised by Nazism during the Weimar era by examining the social characteristics of the membership and leadership of the National Socialist German Workers' Party or Nazi Party (*Nationalsozialistische Deutsche Arbeiterpartei* – NSDAP), and that of a number of its specialist organisations which, along with the party itself, formed the Nazi Movement. The Nazi Party's electoral base will also be reviewed.

It was the dramatic surge in support for the Nazi Party – a marginal force on the fringe of German politics for much of the 1920s – in the *Reichstag* election of 14 September 1930 that first prompted contemporary observers and political analysts to look more closely into the question of *who* were the supporters of Nazism. Much speculation on the social bases of Nazism took place in the 1930s, while the revelation of the full extent of German barbarism following the defeat of the Third Reich gave renewed impetus to diagnosing which social group or groups had provided Nazism with its mass base. Two main hypotheses about the social background of the support mobilised by the Nazis were advanced from the early 1930s onwards which had one major feature in common: they were based on very little, if any, *empirical* evidence. On the basis of impressionistic assertions not founded upon any meaningful evidence, contemporary political commentators, political scientists and historians came to the conclusion that the Nazi Party during its so-called *Kampfzeit* or 'time of struggle' – as the Nazis called the period stretching from the formation of the party in January 1919 to Hitler becoming chancellor on 30 January 1933 – was a middle-class party (*Mittelstandspartei*), or more often specifically a lower-middle-class movement. The view that it was the overwhelming support drawn from the lower middle class that allowed the Nazi Party to become a mass movement by 1933 became the orthodox interpretational approach to be found in virtually all major studies on Nazism published before and after the Second World War. That approach dominated the analysis of the social characteristics of the Nazi Movement until the 1980s. It is still encountered in textbooks – and even specialist literature – on the Nazi phenomenon written in the last two decades, despite the availability of summaries of the results of recent research on the social bases of Nazism in which the veracity of the 'middle-class thesis' is strongly questioned, if not refuted altogether [48; 49; 90; 94; 105; 108; 127; 136]. The counter-argument, which contends the Nazi Party was a people's party (*Volkspartei*) based on support from all social groupings, a hypothesis which also first surfaced in the 1930s, found few supporters at the time and remained very much a minority view in the post-war period until comparatively recently. The fact the Nazis themselves constantly claimed from the 1920s onwards that their party rested on a broad social base, that the Nazi Movement drew support from all social classes and that it was a people's party transcending the class divide, complicated the arguments surrounding the social bases of Nazism, both before and after the collapse of the Nazi state.

Various attempts to develop other theories on the nature of Nazism have also been made over time. The 'Marginal Man' hypothesis, based on the idea that members of the Nazi Party were essentially 'failures' or 'marginal' types, a theory first suggested by Konrad Heiden [60], found some support and was pushed to an absurd level by Daniel Lerner in the post-war period [84]. On the basis of an analysis of 577 biographies of Nazi functionaries included in the 1934 edition of *Das Deutsche Führerlexicon*, Lerner concluded that 56.6 per cent of the Nazi 'elite' were 'marginal'.

Given his strange choice of indices to determine 'marginality' – for Lerner dubbed individuals who married early or late in life, or those who had studied abroad, or those who were artisans, farmers, enlisted men, Bavarians or Catholic, as well as those who were from the Rhineland, as 'marginal' – it is surprising that the percentage he arrived at was not higher still [84: *84–99*]. Lerner never makes clear the criteria he used to select the biographies he analysed from a publication which had been officially approved by the Nazis and one which had a clear propagandistic character. His 'sample' certainly could not be used to substantiate the contention that the 'study confirms the thesis that the Nazi movement was a middle-class and lower-middle class movement . . . the melting pot of the German middle class', as asserted by Franz Neumann in the introduction to Lerner's book [84: *v*]. Jakub Banaszkiewicz combined the 'Marginal Man' theory with the 'middle-class theory' in his investigation of the social bases of Nazism, and reached the conclusion that 'in the emergence and development of the German fascist movement, a dominant role was played mainly by two social groups: the petty bourgeoisie and people of the social fringe' [6: *251*]. The 'Generational Revolt' hypothesis, the view that the 'youth factor' rather than the 'class factor' played the most critical role in mobilising support for Nazism, is another thesis developed to explain the nature of Nazi support, one most forcefully argued by Peter Loewenberg [86] and Peter Merkl [96; 97]. The idea that Nazism represented a form of 'Green Revolt', that it was essentially a small-town and rural phenomenon, has also been advocated over the years by a number of historians [59; 87]. All of these alternative theories, however, have had little impact on the debate on the social characteristics of Nazism, in which the conflicting hypotheses of the 'middle-class party' or 'class party' and 'people's party' or 'mass party' have dominated the scene since the early 1930s, with the former making all the running until the last few decades.

Establishing as accurate a picture of the social bases of the Nazi Movement as possible is, of course, of fundamental importance in any attempt to comprehend the Nazi phenomenon. Given the almost universal acceptance of the thesis that it was essentially a middle-class movement, the main thrust of research from the 1930s onwards was centred on explaining *why* the *Mittelstand* was so partial to Nazism, rather than on providing a firm empirical foundation on which to base the theory. The recognition – primarily in the last three decades or so – that the social bases of Nazism were very much broader, and that the Nazi Movement attracted support from all occupational and social groupings, has stimulated the re-thinking of the *why* question and broadened the scope of analysis to consider factors which drew sections of the working and upper classes to Nazism during the 1920s and early 1930s.

The objective of this book is to review work which has been done on the social background of those individuals who joined the Nazi Movement during the Weimar Republic, a period when German society was trying to adjust to the demands made by an open society, by a pluralist, bourgeois-democratic parliamentary system. The social and occupational background of the 1.6 million who joined the Nazi Party between February and May 1933, when the Nazi Party enforced a temporary recruitment ban, will not be given attention. Undoubtedly many of the *Märzgefallenen* (the 'March Fallen', that is those who joined the NSDAP following its success in securing 43.9 per cent of the vote in the 5 March 1933 *Reichstag* election) and *Maiveilchen* (the 'May Violets', the hundreds of thousands who rushed to join the Nazi Party once it had announced that it was bringing in a temporary halt in recruitment as from 1 May 1933), as the Nazi members of some long-standing disparagingly described the huge flood of individuals who stampeded into the party between February and May 1933, probably represent the influx of diverse social forces prompted perhaps less by conviction than by opportunism or necessity. The social types that swelled the Nazi Party during the Third Reich (by 1939 the NSDAP had around 5.3 million members, and by the end of the war over 8 million) are also left aside. By concentrating on the Weimar era, the focus falls on those individuals who *made a free choice* to support Nazism. The millions who joined the Nazi Party during the Third Reich were undoubtedly characterised by different motives to those who made the decision to support Nazism when it was not a party of government. Obviously the operational environment in which people made their choice to enter the Nazi Party was vastly different before Hitler was appointed chancellor on 30 January 1933 – which signified that the Nazi Party had become a party of government at the national level for the first time – than thereafter.

The same applies to the choice made by those individuals who joined any of the numerous specialist organisations generated by the Nazi Movement before 1933, which targeted the special interests of such diverse elements of German society as blue-collar workers, white-collar employees, shopkeepers, students, women, youth, civil servants, doctors, dentists, teachers, lawyers, farmers and so on. The social characteristics of some of the Nazi specialist organisations, such as those established to recruit farmers, teachers, lawyers and doctors, are obviously relatively clearly defined in class terms. The interesting aspect of such specialist organisations catering for middle- and upper-class elements of German society is the *number* that they mobilised before 1933. However, the social configuration of the membership of such important specialist organisations as the SA (*Sturmabteilung* – Storm Section), the SS (*Schutzstaffel* – Protection Squad), the HJ (*Hitlerjugend* – Hitler Youth) and the NSBO (*Nationalsozialistische Betriebszellenorganisation* – National Socialist Factory Cell Organisation), all of which aimed their appeal at all social classes, is also of critical importance to an understanding of the social configuration of the Nazi Movement as a whole. This is especially pertinent in view of the fact that some of these, such as the SA and the NSBO, attracted individuals who were not invariably members of the NSDAP also. Paralleling the work that has been done on the social characteristics of the membership of the Nazi Party in the last three or so decades, historians and social scientists have also been investigating the social contours of the membership of several of the more significant Nazi specialist organisations. The results of their research will also be reviewed.

Finally, another dimension which explores the social contours of Nazism from a different, though related, perspective to that of membership analysis will be examined: the social characteristics of the Nazi electorate before Germany became a one-party state in 1933. Although in a qualitative sense the analysis of the Nazi electorate does not deal with the committed, hard-core element of the Nazi Movement in the way that membership analysis does, it nevertheless provides a useful additional insight into the nature of the support given by large sections of German society to Nazism before 1933. As in the case of the work that has been done in the last few decades on the social characteristics of the membership of the Nazi Movement, massive strides have been made in the last twenty years or so in identifying the social background of the millions of Germans who voted for the Nazi Party before 1933. This work has replaced the educated guesswork of the past with firm results derived from the increasingly sophisticated quantitative methods that have been employed in interrogating the massive electoral data available to those trying to find an answer to the question: 'Who voted for Hitler?'.

Chapter 2

Historiographical survey

From 1930 onwards – and especially after the Nazi electoral break-through in the *Reichstag* election of 14 September 1930, when the Nazi Party secured 18.3 per cent of the vote – contemporary historians, political scientists and political commentators began to tackle the question of the social bases of Nazism in earnest. Incompatible hypotheses about the social contours of Nazism were developed at the time which were not substantiated by any meaningful or significant empirical data, hypotheses which continued to influence the debate in the post-1945 period, when the question of 'Who supported Nazism' was given new impetus following the revelation of German barbarism during the Third Reich.

The most enduring and widely supported theory of the social bases of Nazism developed in the early 1930s, which was the dominant, orthodox view until at least the 1980s, was the 'middle-class thesis' of Nazism, or often – more specifically – the 'lower-middle-class thesis'. This rests on the notion that the Nazi Party recruited its membership and secured its electorate almost exclusively from the ranks of the petite bourgeoisie. There was generally no differentiation made at first between these two quite distinct aspects of its support. Needless to say, the middle-class or 'bourgeois nature' of National Socialism was orthodoxy among Marxist historians from the outset. The idea that the Nazi virus could affect the working class was anathema to Marxist scholars, who from the 1920s onwards adhered to the view that Nazism was essentially a tool of monopoly capitalism. But support for the middle-class thesis is also widely to be found in the writings of non-Marxists scholars before 1933. It is reflected in a series of articles published between 1931 and 1933 by Werner Stephan, who analysed the local, regional and national election results of the early 1930s and pointed to the successes which the Nazi Party achieved in predominantly Protestant middle-class urban and rural areas [128–31]. Stephan saw the collapse of the vote of the middle-class parties in the early 1930s as *the* factor which fuelled the rise of the electoral strength of the Nazi Party. He took it for certain that the loss of support in the *Reichstag* elections of the early 1930s collectively suffered by the German Democratic Party, the German People's Party and the German National People's Party – parties which he assumed were supported at the polls virtually exclusively by the *Mittelstand* – was the factor which accounted for the rise of the Nazi Party [129: *576*]. He also looked at the performance of the Nazis in predominantly working-class, middle-class and upper-class districts of a number of cities, demonstrating that in the working-class districts of the towns which he investigated the Nazi vote was low, while in predominantly middle-class districts it was often very high [128: *797*]. Also very influential in the entrenchment of the middle-class thesis in the early 1930s was Theodor Geiger, who put the success of the Nazis in the *Reichstag* election of September 1930 down to a 'Panic in the *Mittelstand*' [50]. In his seminal work on the class structure of German society published in 1932, which included a chapter on the relationship between Nazism and the *Mittelstand* [51: *109–22*], Geiger claimed that it was 'a known fact that the NSDAP was based on recruits drawn from both the old and the new *Mittelstand*' [51: *112*]. He underpinned his view by reference to electoral statistics on the Nazi vote and observations made by political commentators. Similar conclusions, again not substantiated by any meaningful evidence, were reached by the American political scientist Harold D. Lasswell, who argued Nazism represented little more than a reactionary movement of the lower middle class responding to the threat of big business and organised labour [83]. Influential also in popularising the middle-class thesis of Nazism was Konrad Heiden, whose pioneering study of the Nazi Party was published in New York in 1935 [60]. Heiden asserted that 'the Nazis were a class party' and 'that the membership was drawn primarily from the lower middle class' [60: *18, 28*].

The first empirically based investigation on the social characteristics of the Nazi Party was published in 1938 by the American sociologist Theodore Abel [1]. This was based on 683 replies supplied by Nazis who had responded to an essay competition entitled 'Why

I became a National Socialist', which Abel had organised in 1934 with the co-operation of the Nazi press in the Hesse region, a competition which was open to those Nazi members who had joined the party before 1 January 1933. Abel discarded eighty-three accounts, including all of the forty-eight replies received from women, whom Abel viewed as atypical, distorting the male Nazi Movement as he saw it. On the basis of this unrepresentative sample, Abel argued that the NSDAP was a lower-middle-class affair. Similar conclusions were reached by Hans Gerth in his article on the membership and leadership of the Nazi Party which appeared in 1940 [53]. Using data which had appeared in a Nazi history of the party, as well as some data on the social background of its membership published in the Nazi press, Gerth pointed to the under-representation of the working class and of farmers, and the significant over-representation of white-collar employees and independents in the Nazi membership.

In the post-war era the (lower-) middle-class thesis was supported and refined in a number of important studies in which conclusions on the social profile of the Nazi Party were usually still made on the basis of a cursory review of the Nazi electorate. A strong supporter of the middle-class thesis of Nazism in the post-war era was the American sociologist Seymour Martin Lipset, who argued that 'classic fascism' was the movement of the petite bourgeoisie radicalised by the fear of capitalism and organised labour, the product of economic crisis and of the long-term consequences of industrialisation [85]. Variants of the middle-class thesis are to be found in the works of a number of scholars who wrote influential books on Nazism from the 1950s to the 1970s, important studies which shaped subsequent work on the phenomenon. Thus Karl Dietrich Bracher, who was much concerned with the question of why the *Mittelstand* was so attracted to the NSDAP, characterised it as 'a middle-class mass party' [16: *187–8, 195–204*]. Dietrich Orlow pointed to the 'lower-middle-class origins' of the 'pioneer' group of the Nazi Party [111: *47*]. Martin Broszat also saw the sociological picture of the Nazi Party very much in lower-middle-class terms [17: *29–32*], while Francis Carsten argued that it was the '*petit-bourgeois* standards and resentments' of white-collar workers, civil servants, farmers and independent businessmen which made them particularly susceptible to the appeal of Nazism [23: *143*]. Little, if any, empirical evidence was advanced to substantiate the middle-class image of Nazism portrayed in these works. It was taken as axiomatic by the vast majority of scholars working on Nazism that the question of the class nature of Nazism had already been conclusively answered.

Given the almost universal acceptance before the Second World War – and for many decades thereafter – of the hypothesis that Nazism was a middle-class phenomenon, the comparatively few scholars and political scientists, who argued from the 1930s onwards that the Nazi Party was a people's party able to mobilise support from all class groupings in German society, had little impact. The German political scientist Gerhard Friters, studying in the United States in the early 1930s, suggested that although the Nazi Party and the SA were based largely on support derived from white-collar employees and the independent urban and rural *Mittelstand* (as well as students in the case of the SA), the Nazis were also able to attract younger age cohorts of the working class, which he estimated as constituting between 10 and 15 per cent of the NSDAP's membership [47]. Similar conclusions were reached by Hans Jäger, who also emphasised the Nazi Party's middle-class nature, but pointed to the significant section of unemployed and young workers among the party's membership, with workers predominating in the SA [66: *1430–1*]. Sigmund Neumann, while viewing the NSDAP as primarily a party of the *Mittelstand*, noted the support it secured from youth, from elements of the elite (from the high-ranking military, the aristocracy and higher civil servants), as well as from the working class. He argued that it was the 'broad social foundation' on which the Nazi Party was based by 1932, which – despite fluctuations in the extent of its support – gave it its constant strength [106, *78–82*]. In his analysis of the rise of Hitler, the future president of the Federal Republic, Theodor Heuss, noted 'the strong contingent of working-class people' which was to be found in the Nazi Party by the early 1930s and pointed to the heterogeneity of its membership [62: *163*]. Significantly, the argument that the NSDAP had a broad social base was voiced even by a few socialists, notably Paul Sering, who came to the conclusion that the NSDAP 'recruited from members of all classes', including the working class [122]. Support for the view of the Nazi Party as a 'people's party' is also to be found in the post-war period, most notably in Reinhard Bendix's early work on the theme, which argued that the Nazi membership was 'quite heterogeneous' and described the NSDAP as a *Volkspartei* [8]. In his analysis of the relationship existing between the *Mittelstand* and Nazism, Heinrich August Winkler reached the conclusion – based on electoral data and the Nazi Party's membership census of 1935 – that although the middle class dominated the party, a not insignificant presence of workers within the NSDAP justified calling it a *Volkspartei* [134–6].

Given the enormous strides which have been made in the publication of empirical data on the social bases of Nazism since the 1970s, the very limited evidence on which the debate on the sociology of the Nazi Movement was conducted for forty years is astonishing. Until the power of the computer and of ecological regression analysis was systematically used in researching which social groups supported the Nazi Party at the polls, historians and social scientists had only been in the position of reaching – at best – somewhat tentative conclusions about the social characteristics of the Nazi electorate. As far as the membership of the Nazi Party was concerned, there was only the limited material gathered by Abel at the outset of the Third Reich. In the post-war period one known detailed analysis on the sociology of the membership of the NSDAP first became available to historians, the *Partei-Statistik*, a membership census undertaken by the Nazis themselves (see Figure 1), which was distributed among the party cadre – but restricted to internal party use only – by the Reich Organisation Leader Robert Ley in 1935 [113]. Once it became available to historians and social scientists, this data set – as one might expect, given its provenance – was treated with great suspicion and more often than not dismissed as a piece of Nazi propaganda, or as a reflection of wishful thinking on the part of the Nazi leadership. The aspect of the *Partei-Statistik* which proved particularly contentious was the data it contained on the level of working-class support the party had managed to acquire before January 1933, which buttressed the claim made by the Nazis that their party was a genuine people's party transcending the class divide. For though the *Partei-Statistik* pointed to a strong presence of the *Mittelstand* within the ranks of the NSDAP, it also noted that 'workers' made up 31.5 per cent of the membership recruited by the party between the end of February 1925 and the end of January 1933 [113: *70*]. Since the *Partei-Statistik* also provided

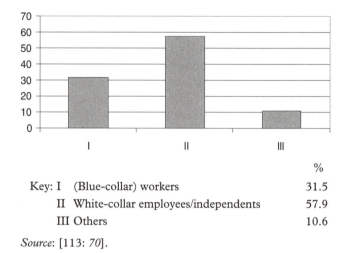

	%
Key: I (Blue-collar) workers	31.5
II White-collar employees/independents	57.9
III Others	10.6

Source: [113: *70*].

Figure 1   The occupational status of the membership of the Nazi Party on 30 January 1933 according to the *Partei-Statistik* (N: 849,009)

the breakdown of the party membership at the *Gau* (or regional) level, it also threw much light on the regional variations of the social make-up of the party. The extent of working-class support present in the party before 1933, for example, ranged from a low of 24 per cent in *Gau* Greater Berlin to a high of 43.8 per cent in *Gau* Westphalia-South [113: *148*]. The veracity of the percentages given in the census for the working-class membership at the national and *Gau* level was usually denied by those who adhered to the 'middle-class movement' thesis. Questions about the representative nature and reliability of the data were raised. The 'class model' employed in the analysis was queried. Another line of attack was to suggest that the percentage of workers in the party is meaningless, because the Nazis failed to define what they meant by 'workers' [26: *253*].

In fact, the Nazi statisticians did make some attempt to define what they meant by the various categories they used in the census, such as 'workers', 'white-collar workers' and 'self-employed'. The 'workers' category comprised the occupational groups of unskilled workers, agricultural workers, workers in the mining industry and skilled workers [113: *55*], an approach broadly in line with that employed by national census statisticians of the time. The real problem

with the *Partei-Statistik* is that it can only show the social composition of the membership as on 1 January 1935. It cannot give an
accurate picture of the social characteristics of the party's membership for the period from February 1925 to 30 January 1933 because
it records only those individuals who had joined and re-joined the
Nazi Party in 1925 or thereafter who were still in the party at the time
the census was taken. The problem here is that while the Nazis had
enrolled around 1.5 million members before 30 January 1933, only
849,009 of these were still in the party at the time the census was
taken [113: *12*]. The *Partei-Statistik* cannot, therefore, tell us any-
thing about the approximately 650,000 Germans (and Austrians,
who were also enrolled by Munich party headquarters) who had
joined the party before 30 January 1933 and were no longer in the
party by the time of the membership count of 1934.

However, despite this real limitation, there are a number of factors which suggest that the *Partei-Statistik* does represent a genuine
attempt by the Nazis to get an insight into the social background of
their membership. What sways one towards this view is that the data
was never published during the Third Reich, nor used in Nazi propaganda to provide hard evidence to substantiate the claim that the
party was an authentic trans-class party in which all social groupings
were represented. What motivated the Nazis to find out what sort
of social profile their membership had is made clear in the pream-
ble to the *Partei-Statistik*: it was to be used to work out the future
recruitment strategy of the party once the ban on recruitment was
(initially partially) lifted in 1935. The Nazis admitted that workers were not present in the party in sufficient numbers, and that the
recruitment of workers in general – and miners, agricultural labourers and forestry workers in particular – was to be pursued once the
bar on further recruitment was lifted [113: *65*]. The Nazis were
aware that the *Mittelstand* was over-represented within the ranks of
the party membership and admitted that workers and farmers were
under-represented in the party, whereas white-collar employees, independents and civil servants were over-represented [113: *56*]. If,
as has been suggested, the Nazis were intent on distorting the facts,
they did not do a very good job in manipulating the data they collected. It would have been relatively easy for them to have massaged
the figures for the various social groupings present in the party to
bring them more in line with the class structure of German society.

Because the *Partei-Statistik* was for many decades in the post-war period the only major source available on the sociography of the Nazi Party, and since it also provided a breakdown of the party membership at the *Gau* or regional level, it proved an irresistible source to historians dealing with the social characteristics of the Nazi Party's rank-and-file at the national level [17; 119], and especially to those historians who pioneered studies dealing with the development of the Nazi Party at the regional level, though these invariably used this source with reservation and great care, if not with considerable misgivings [15; 55; 107; 114; 118].

As long as empirical evidence on the occupational and social background of the membership of the NSDAP was basically confined to the disputed data available in the *Partei-Statistik*, the generally accepted notion of the Nazi Party as a middle-class movement was relatively easy to sustain, as was its corollary that the members it was able to recruit from the working class and upper class were marginal at best. The turning point in the debate came in the 1970s when two developments occurred which placed the controversy surrounding the social characteristics of the Nazi Movement on to an increasingly firm *empirical* footing: new data was discovered and – along with known electoral and membership data – subjected to computer analysis. Developments in computer technology facilitated the use of a major *known* source [18; 123], the around 10 million NSDAP membership files housed until the early 1990s in the American-controlled Berlin Document Center (hereafter BDC). Stored in roughly 5,000 boxes, the Nazi Party membership cards issued between 1925 and 1945, which fell by chance into American hands in 1945, were originally divided into two sets, the Blue File arranged geographically by *Gau* (estimated to contain 7.6–7.8 million cards), and the Green File arranged alphabetically by surname (the Master File of the membership of the NSDAP, containing around 4.4 million membership cards). In the war crimes trials and de-nazification processes after the war, the Blue File was unfortunately (for those interested in the social profile of the Nazi Party at the regional level) also rearranged alphabetically. The first scholars to draw samples from this massive holding and publish their results using computer analysis were Michael Kater [75] and Paul Madden [91]. In more recent years a joint research project undertaken by William Brustein and Jürgen Falter [21] also involved sampling this source. The Master File of the NSDAP's membership has provided very rich results, especially on the longitudinal development pattern of the social contours of the membership of the Nazi Party. In the course of the 1970s and 1980s the approximately 260,000 individual SA files (around two-thirds of these relate to Bavaria, which limits the utility of this source) compiled by the BDC were used by Conan Fischer [41–3], Mathilde Jamin [68], Eric Reiche [116] and Bruce Campbell [22] in their research on the membership and leadership of the SA. The SS personnel files, which the BDC also houses, have been sampled by Gunnar Boehnert [13–14] and Herbert Ziegler [137] in their examination of the leadership of the SS.

Additional to the use of these known sources, the discovery of extensive data on the membership of the Nazi Party (and to a lesser extent on a number of its specialist organisations, primarily the SA and SS) in numerous archives throughout Germany – in the form of branch membership records and lists of newly enrolled members at the local and regional level – rapidly expanded the source base on the membership of the Nazi Movement, which made it possible to reach firm conclusions about its social structure. Material available in the Hoover Microfilm Collection of the NSDAP *Hauptarchiv*, namely the membership list entitled 'Adolf Hitler's Comrades-in-Arms' (*Adolf Hitlers Mitkämpfer*), which records all those individuals who had joined the party – virtually all of the members were resident in Munich – between 1919 and 1921, as well as membership lists relating to Nazi branches established in the early 1920s at Rosenheim, Passau, Landshut, Mannheim, Ingolstadt and Berchtesgaden, was used by Donald Douglas [29], Madden [88], Kater [75: *242–3*], and Detlef Mühlberger [101: *54–6*]. A fragment of the pre-November 1923 national membership register of the NSDAP, which records some 4,800 members who had joined the party in the six weeks or so before the abortive Munich Putsch of 9 November 1923, was also unearthed and provided the basis for a pioneering piece of research on the social structure of the party's early membership by Kater [70]. In the 1970s and early 1980s further data came to light on the membership of a number of Nazi branches active in the Ruhr in the mid-1920s [75: *246, 248*; 101: *78–80*], as well as on various branches scattered around Germany, such as those in Hamburg, Brunswick, Starnberg and Königsberg [75: *246*]. In 1978 Lawrence

Stokes published a very detailed study on the Nazi branch at Eutin, demonstrating the variable social configuration of its membership, as well as throwing light on the social background of the SA recruited in the area [132]. Studies on the social structure of the Nazi Party at the regional level, such as those on Saxony [104] and on the Border Province Posen-West Prussia [100], and at the county and local level, such as those on the Wetzlar region [39], on the city of Munich [5] and on the town of Offenbach [81], have all been added in recent years. A number of critical studies on the question of the social composition of the Nazi electorate have also been published in the last two decades by Richard Hamilton [56], Thomas Childers [26], Dirk Hänisch [57] and Falter [33], along with studies by Fischer [43] and Jamin [68] on the membership and leadership of the party's largest specialist organisation, the SA. In the course of the 1980s and 1990s the discovery of new sources turned into a flood, and the known sources housed in the BDC were used more extensively. A series of further studies were published on the membership of the Nazi Party by Mühlberger [102] and by Brustein [20], and on the social origins of the SS leadership by Ziegler [137]. Additional material dealing with the social background of the SA by Richard Bessel [9: *33–45*], by Mühlberger [101: *114–22*; 102: *159–80*] and by Fischer and Mühlberger [45] also became available, while the top brass of the SA was subjected to further analysis by Campbell [22]. The rank-and-file of the SS was also subjected to the first detailed statistical analyses by Mühlberger [102: *181–201*] and by Anne Becker and Mühlberger [7]. Finally, the first data on the social structure of the NSBO's membership recruited in the Berlin region was made available by Volker Kratzenberg [80]. Collectively these studies have revolutionised our understanding of the social forces on which the Nazi Movement rested.

Chapter 3

Methodological problems

Once empirical evidence began to be used in the debate on the social make-up of Nazism from the 1970s onwards, a number of methodological problems rapidly emerged. Far from allowing historians and social scientists to reach a consensus view on the social bases of Nazism, the use of existing and new data produced – interwoven with the 'middle-class' versus 'people's party' dispute – some lively debates about how to handle data of variable quality and provenance. Three major problems faced the researcher working on the social bases of Nazism. First, the limitations inherent in the very nature of the data on the basis of which conclusions had to be drawn about the social characteristics of Nazism. Secondly, the difficulties which arose in the assignment of various occupations to specific occupational groupings and their placement in turn into social class categories. And thirdly, the question of the representative nature of the data being evaluated.

All of the macro, and the majority of the micro, analyses of the social configuration of the individuals who joined the Nazi Party available to date depend on membership lists or individual membership cards which usually provide the researcher with information on the surname, first name (from which gender can be established), date of birth, place of birth, 'occupation' (*Beruf*) or 'estate' (*Stand*), the place of residence of the individual, the name of the party branch to which the individual belonged, the date when he or she joined the NSDAP, along with – in the majority of cases – the membership number issued by Munich party headquarters. Basically all that is available for the purpose of establishing the social status of the Nazi members is what he or she entered under 'occupation' or 'estate'. Generally lacking is the type of comprehensive information which is normally required for contemporary social class analysis, such as details relating to the family background, education, income level and financial status of the individuals involved [102: *11*]. A further limitation is that it is on the basis of the *self-assigned occupational description* given that the individual's position in social space has to be determined, and that creates a number of difficulties [4; 52: *41*; 120]. There is generally no sure way of checking if the members inflated their occupational status or distorted their position in some way or other. Nor do we know if the members put down the occupations for which they were trained rather than the occupation they happened to be exercising at the time of their entry into the party. Nor do we usually have any indication as to whether they were actually employed at the time of entry. Nor can we know that if they were temporarily unemployed they simply put down the last occupation they happened to have held, or even the occupation to which they aspired.

There is a partial – but laborious and time-consuming – control on the veracity of what individuals entered under 'occupation': that provided by town and county address books. These were published annually and recorded the occupation of the heads of households in towns and villages throughout Germany. The problem here is that the great bulk of the members who joined the Nazi Movement before 1933 – and on this point there is unanimity among scholars – were very young [76; 89], and therefore unlikely to have already established their own household. According to the *Partei-Statistik*, some 70 per cent of the 849,009 members in the party on 30 January 1933 were under forty years of age, of which 42.2 per cent were under the age of thirty [113: *162*].

It is likely that an individual joining a Nazi Party branch before 1933, and especially before 1930, a time when most branches were not particularly large, would have joined a group in which the majority of the members would have known each other, and in which the branch leader would know or get to know – or could check – the background of the applicant. Given this 'control' aspect, it is likely that the occupational titles cited on membership application forms were relatively accurate. Admittedly, this type of control was more difficult to sustain in the period of rapid membership growth in the early 1930s, notably in the more sizeable branches established in the larger towns and cities. Less of a problem is the information on occupational status contained in the lists of Nazi activists and of rank-and-file members of the party (and especially of the SA and SS) compiled by the police in various parts of Germany. It can be assumed that in these the job titles given by the Nazis subjected to interrogation were generally accurate since it is less likely that a party member subjected to police interrogations would have falsified his or her occupational title, given that these were open to verification. In small towns or villages, moreover, those asking the questions more often than not probably knew the individuals personally.

Police records usually provide much more information on the individuals under investigation, and often provide details on their parental background, marital status, religion and record of employment, occasionally also including the name of their employer. More detailed still is the information contained in SA and SS membership files. These generally record not only the occupation exercised by an individual at the time of his application to join the organisation, but also the occupation for which he had trained. The income level of the individual is often also noted. In SA and SS files all sorts of additional data was entered as a matter of course, such as the member's date of application to join the SA or SS; his date of promotion and record of rank reached; his military record; the medals he had been awarded if he had seen active service; details on his war-wounds; his Free Corps membership and service; information on whether he had been in the police service and the rank he had reached; details on the size of his family (including information on the age and gender of any children); his driving licence details; the date on which he had joined the Nazi Party; his party membership number; details relating to party offices held; the number of Party Rallies he had attended; if he had a police record, and if so, a list of his offence(s). Recorded also were his height, shoe and hat size! Not infrequently the personal files of SA and SS members also contain a life history (*Lebenslauf*) of the member from which an insight into his educational background, occupational training, periods of employment and unemployment and membership of other political and non-political organisations can be obtained.

Allied to the problem of the accuracy of self-assigned occupational description is that some of the 'occupations' cited by applicants are terminologically imprecise. This is certainly so as regards the most frequently encountered ones, namely 'worker' (*Arbeiter*), 'farmer' (*Landwirt*, less frequently *Bauer*) and 'merchant' (*Kaufmann*). The description 'worker' is imprecise in that this could apply to an unskilled, semi-skilled or skilled worker, a craftsman in a dependent position, an agricultural worker, a blue-collar worker in the public sector or a domestic worker. Even a dependent white-collar worker in a low status position might occasionally have described himself simply as a 'worker'. A number of historians suggest that many self-assigned occupations listed in Nazi membership records were at times far removed from social reality. That the word 'merchant' often lacked precision is certainly borne out by some examples cited by Johnpeter Horst Grill in his study on the NSDAP in Baden [55]. Using additional information on individual members who described themselves as 'merchant', he found that the term was used by a 'terminated clerk', an 'insurance clerk', a 'small machine factory owner', a 'quarry owner' and even in one case by a 'drifter' [55: *84*]. Christoph Schmidt examined data provided by long-term members of the NSDAP recruited in Hesse and compared it with the evidence on these members to be found in the BDC [120]. He came to the conclusion that the occupational descriptions they gave in their 'Old Guard' accounts were more often than not misleading [120: *22–6*]. Herbert Andrews also points to discrepancies in the accounts of the Hesse Old Guard when it came to their occupations in comparison with their membership cards housed in the BDC, but argues that the BDC holdings are sufficiently accurate to allow generalised conclusions to be made from the register of the membership cards about the social bases of the Nazi Movement [4: *307*].

It is an unfortunate fact that except in relatively rare instances where full data on Nazi members is available – and that is primarily restricted to the leadership corps of the Nazi Party and the heads of its diverse specialist organisations – the goal of absolute precision is not attainable, and in the absence of totally accurate and detailed information, historians and social scientists are forced to fall back on the data contained in membership cards and membership lists. The occupations of individual Nazis that appear in these sources represent, as Professor Madden has so aptly put it, 'our most important clue to the social composition of the NSDAP' and are, 'in short, . . . the only game in town' [88: *42*].

An area given over to even more theoretical and conceptual conflict relates to the construction of occupational and class models. While there is general consensus on the broad division of German society in the 1920s and 1930s into lower, middle and upper strata, the literature dealing with the social characteristics of Nazism reflects differences in the way historians and social scientists define the strata and the parameters of the social class groupings. Here the decisions made in the assignment of various occupations to specific occupational groups and the placement of these individual groups into social class groupings are critical. A basic problem which bedevilled the analyses of the social characteristics of the Nazi Movement for a long time was the lack of an agreed class model to which scholars working on the theme could all subscribe. As long as class and occupational models were employed which, for example, restricted the working class to just unskilled workers, or which placed all artisans into the *Mittelstand*, there were bound to be major statistical differences in the results obtained from analysing Nazi membership data. Fortunately, the major differences in the class and occupational models used in the past by historians and social scientists working on the sociology of Nazism were removed to a considerable extent in the course of the 1980s and early 1990s. The models currently in use do not, with the exception of that employed by Paul Madden (who in two important publications of the 1980s on the social structure of the Nazi Party's membership continued to place all artisans into the middle class), show major differences (see Tables 1–4).

Given the many objective and subjective determinants which are involved in defining class and class boundaries, there is plenty of room for disagreement. It is clear that differences in the class model employed can produce quite different results from the same set of data. This was illustrated long ago by Theodor Geiger who – on the basis of the occupational data provided in the 1925 census – produced two quite different class models for Weimar Germany. In his first model the criterion he used to determine classification was a purely economic one, namely income and property (*Besitzstufe*). The most striking result of this approach was the extraordinary percentage found under the 'workers' category, which alone accounted for 74.77 per cent of the working population, while those deemed to belong to the *Mittelstand* accounted for only 24.39 per cent (the

Table 1 *Social ranking and occupational distribution according to Kater*

Lower class
Unskilled workers
Skilled (craft) workers
Other skilled workers
Lower middle class
Master craftsmen (independent)
Non-academic professionals
Lower and intermediate (petty) employees
Lower and intermediate (petty) civil servants
Merchants (self-employed)
Farmers (self-employed)
Elite
Managers
Higher civil servants
Academic professionals
Students (university and upper school)
Entrepreneurs

Source: [75: *241*].

remaining 0.84 per cent were classified by him as 'capitalists') [51: *72*]. When Geiger measured what he termed the 'socio-ideological' structure of German society, in which occupation and 'mentality' determined the classification, the category 'workers', now renamed 'proletariat', was reduced to 51.03 per cent, while members of the 'Old' and 'New' *Mittelstand* accounted for 18.33 and 13.76 per cent respectively. The percentage for 'capitalists' remained constant in the model, but a further 13.76 per cent of the membership was now assigned to a new social grouping suspended between the working and middle classes, the 'proletaroid', as Geiger called it [51: *73*].

In the 1960s and 1970s, when the first quantitative analysis of the social background of the Nazi Party's membership based on *empirical* data began to appear, attention initially fell on the support the results gave to the 'orthodox' middle-class thesis of Nazism, rather than the methodologies employed in the utilisation of the data. Neither Georg Franz-Willing [46] nor Werner Maser [95], both of whom discovered and examined fragments of membership

Table 2 *Social ranking and occupational distribution according to Madden*

Proletariat
Agricultural labourers
Semi-skilled and unskilled labourers
Servants
Military (enlisted)
Skilled labourers

Mittelstand
Artisans
White collar
Small business
Students
Arts
Farmers
Managers and senior officials
Military (officers)
Professions

Upper middle class and upper class
Capitalists, industrialists, large landowners, persons with private incomes

Others
Unemployed
Housewives
Retired

Source: [88: *43*].

lists on the early NSDAP, seemingly gave much thought to the way they handled the material. Although their conclusions about the social profile of the Nazi Party membership – in their eyes it was a lower-middle-class phenomenon – had the merit of being based on original calculations resting on albeit limited primary sources, the methodologies they employed were quite primitive. For example, in the occupational classification model adopted by Maser, shopkeepers were placed into three different occupational categories, while no differentiation was made between dependent and independent artisans [95: *254–5*]. Franz-Willing had some rather odd ideas as to what constituted the occupational category of 'free professions' (*freie Berufe*), into which – among other diverse

Table 3 *Social ranking and occupational distribution according to Mühlberger*

Lower class
Agricultural workers
Unskilled and semi-skilled workers
Skilled (craft) workers
Other skilled workers
Domestic workers

Lower and middle middle class
Master craftsmen
Non-academic professionals
White-collar employees
Lower civil servants
Merchants
Farmers

Upper middle class and upper class
Managers
Higher civil servants
University students
Academic professionals
Entrepreneurs

Status unclear
Non-university students
Pensioners/retired
Wives/widows
Military personnel
Illegible/no data

Source: [102: *20–5*].

occupations – he placed both bank personnel and salesmen [46: *129–30*].

Kater, in his pioneering work on the sociology of Nazism in the 1970s, produced data which also strongly reinforced the 'orthodox' middle-class thesis of Nazism, an interpretation to which he was clearly committed until the 1990s [70–5]. In his early work on the social characteristics of the supporters of Nazism, Kater obtained very low percentage values for the size of the working-class membership of the NSDAP (and the same applies to his analysis of SA

Table 4 *Social ranking and occupational distribution according to Brustein and Falter*

Working class
Workers with specialised skills engaged directly in production process
Workers with specialised skills supporting the production process
Other workers
Domestic servants

Old middle class
Owners, self-employed and entrepreneurs
Administrators, directors, managers and high level civil servants
Door-to-door or street peddlers
Assisting dependants

New middle class
White-collar technical employees, civil servants and specialised staff
Foremen and supervisory staff
Commercial employees, administrative officials and office personnel

Without occupation

Source: [20: *187*].

membership data) because of his use of a class model in which he only included unskilled workers in the working-class category (see Figure 2, Model A). Kater's placement in the 1970s of skilled workers and artisans and their apprentices into the *Mittelstand* naturally inflated the lower-middle-class element supporting the Nazi Party [70]. A similarly narrow definition of the working class was also used by William Sheridan Allen in his classic local study of the development of the Nazi Party in Northeim, though he added 'semi-skilled workers' to the 'unskilled workers' category to define the working class [2: *15*]. In all of his important contributions to the examination of the social bases of the Nazi Party, Paul Madden, a strong advocate of the people's party thesis, has consistently placed artisans – irrespective of whether these are of dependent or independent status – into the *Mittelstand*, thereby reducing the force of his argument that the Nazi Party recruited significant support from the working class [88; 91].

Unsatisfactory also from the methodological perspective is the reverse process of expanding the working class by blurring the differences between manual workers, skilled craftsmen and white-collar

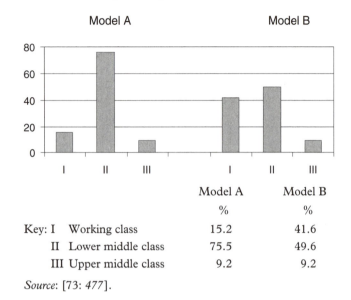

Source: [73: 477].

Figure 2   *Kater's alternative models of the social ranking of individuals joining the Nazi Party between 1925 and 1932* (N: 2,186)

employees (*Angestellte*). Harold Gordon included sections of the latter category, such as clerical workers with limited incomes, store clerks and lower government officials, in the working class [54: 72–3]. Problematic also is the confused definition of the occupational types constituting the working class offered by Donald Douglas, who placed what he describes as 'unskilled white-collar workers' (primarily retail store sales clerks) into the working class, but put artisans (identified as fitters, machinists, metal smiths, printers, electricians, mechanics) into the *Mittelstand* [29: 66].

It is the problem of where to draw the boundary between the working class and the middle class which has created the most difficulties for those working on the sociology of Nazism. It is this question which has been given more than passing consideration when it comes to discussions of the methodological issues surrounding the debate on the social make-up of Nazi support. In his analysis of the many pitfalls awaiting the historian when processing membership data of the Nazi Party, Jürgen Genuneit wrestled particularly with the problem of which occupational sub-groups can be assigned to the working class in the Weimar era [52]. He came up with three possible models. In the first he restricted the working class to 'casual workers, unskilled workers and specialised workers'. Using this minimalist approach, Genuneit calculated that only 6 per cent of the 8,059 individuals contained in his data – derived from fragments of Nazi membership lists relating to the early years of the NSDAP stretching from the autumn of 1919 to the autumn of 1923 – fall into that class. In his second model he added workers who 'perform a service function' (*Dienstleistung*), as a consequence of which workers now accounted for 9 per cent in his data. Finally, when he combined casual workers, unskilled workers, workers with a service function and specialist (skilled) workers, the extent of the working-class membership jumped to 28 per cent. It is this broader definition of the working class, as employed in the 1920s and early 1930s by the government statisticians, which Genuneit uses in the final breakdown of his data [52: 52–6, 59].

It is the placement of dependent craftsmen or artisans which is the most critical and significant factor in explaining the often marked differences in the size of the working and middle classes in the Weimar era in the various class models used by scholars in the debate surrounding the social structure of the Nazi Movement. The placement of 'artisans' into the *Mittelstand* – a feature of Madden's work on the social basis of the Nazi Party (see Table 2), as well as of Kater's early work on the theme – is unrealistic since it seriously distorts the social realities of the Weimar era and significantly reduces the size of the working class in German society in the inter-war years. It runs counter to the concept of the working class employed by German government statisticians who produced the 1925 and 1933 censuses, who placed skilled workers and dependent craftsmen, as well as apprentices, into the working class [103: 51]. It would be unwise to ignore the advice offered by the government statisticians of the time, given their proximity to the social and historical context of the Weimar era and their experience in the field of occupational classification. According to the censuses of 1925 and 1933 unskilled, semi-skilled and skilled workers (a category which includes craftsmen, artisans and their apprentices) made up 46 and 46.3 per cent of the working population of Germany respectively. Just under two-thirds of these were semi-skilled and skilled workers, almost three-quarters of whom were skilled [103: 50–1]. That the placement of all craftsmen and artisans in the *Mittelstand* is not tenable and is inappropriate for the Weimar era is suggested by the fact that dependent skilled workers, craftsmen and artisans, such as toolmakers, locksmiths, bricklayers, joiners, fitters, smiths, painters, plumbers, machinists and lathe-operators, not only made up a large percentage of the German workforce, but were prominent among the membership of both major left-wing parties in Weimar Germany, the Social Democratic Party of Germany (*Sozialdemokratische Partei Deutschlands* – SPD) and the Communist Party of Germany (*Kommunistische Partei Deutschlands* – KPD). Placing all dependent skilled workers, craft workers and artisans into the lower middle class would have a profound impact on the social profile of both the SPD and KPD, giving these working-class parties a significant middle-class base, for according to the SPD's own membership analysis of the occupational status of its membership in 1930, semi-skilled and skilled workers accounted for 53 per cent of its support, while the category 'skilled workers' provided 40 per cent of the membership of the KPD according to its own party census of 1927 [102: *219*].

Kater – undoubtedly influenced by the criticism directed against his very narrow definition of the occupational groups comprising the working class in the Weimar Republic [67] – had second thoughts as to the placement of dependent artisans and craftsmen in the occupational and class model which he employed in his later work on the sociology of the membership and leadership of the Nazi Party (see Figure 2, Model B). That decision – as is reflected in a comparison between the results obtained from the same data analysed according to his first and second 'Class Models' in Figure 2 – had important consequences for the class composition of the Nazi membership which he had sampled in the BDC.

The inclusion of dependent artisans in the working class, however, leads to the problem of how one can determine whether an artisan or craftsman has dependent or independent status. Kater resolved the issue by automatically assigning 36.6 per cent of all artisans to the *Mittelstand* on the assumption that these were self-employed and thus of independent status, placing the rest in the working class on the assumption that they were in a dependent position: a neat solution at first glance, but one which ignores a number of difficulties. We know from the information contained in the 1933 census that the chances of artisans becoming independent in their status (by becoming self-employed) differed widely between the various artisanal occupations, depending on such variables as the capital requirements for setting up an independent business, the method of production and the extent of consumer demand. Only 4.1 per cent of the 799,833 toolmakers (*Schloßer*), numerically the largest single artisanal occupation recorded in the 1933 census, managed to secure independent status, given that their capital outlay to secure that status was comparatively high. At the other extreme, 57.7 per cent of all shoe-makers and cobblers (*Schuhmacher*) and 53.2 per cent of all clock-makers and watch-repairers (*Uhrmacher*), whose capital outlay was comparatively low, reached independent status during their working life. According to the evidence provided in the 1933 census some artisans, such as tailors, hairdressers and butchers, had a one-in-two to one-in-three chance of securing independent status, while others, such as brewers, bookbinders, bricklayers and masons, had a one-in-ten to one-in-twenty chance of setting up their own business [102: *16*]. Crucial therefore, given the widely differing possibilities of becoming independent open to artisans, is the frequency of the artisanal occupations within the working population, measured against the frequency of their appearance in the Nazi membership. On the latter aspect Andrews' analysis of 603 individuals who joined the Nazi Party between 1925 and 1928 is instructive. He found that only 23 (13.3 per cent) of the 172 craftsmen in his data were 'masters or self-employed craftsmen' [4: *312*]. Kater's automatic '36.6 per cent rule' does not take into consideration this frequency aspect. Nor does his approach make allowance for the impact of the age factor. The 1925 census returns show clearly that comparatively few bakers, butchers, locksmiths, painters, cobblers, carpenters etc. under the age of thirty, and not that significant a percentage of those under the age of forty, managed to secure independent status [102: *16–17*]. Given that 70 per cent of the membership of the Nazi Party enumerated in the *Partei-Statistik* were under forty years of age, it is highly probable that the bulk of the artisans who joined the Nazi Movement were also under forty years of age, and that relatively few of these would have had independent status. A way round this problem, one which Mühlberger has consistently employed in his work on the social bases of the Nazi Movement, is to resort to the hierarchic aspect of whether or not an artisan had acquired his master (*Meister*) title. If an individual is entered, for example, as a 'master baker' (*Bäckermeister*) on a Nazi membership list, or if his independent status is indicated in some other way, such as being described as a proprietor of a bakery, he is placed into the master-craftsmen sub-group and assigned to the *Mittelstand* [102: *17*]. Given the status consciousness of the average German at that time, blue-collar worker and white-collar employee alike, it is fairly certain that, as Fischer suggests, an independent artisan only rarely omitted 'to describe himself as a master or make his independent status perfectly clear in some other way in his job description' [43: *19*].

Obviously if an error is made in the assignment of an individual occupation to one occupational sub-group rather than another within the same social class it is not as critical as if mistakes are made in assigning particular occupations to occupational sub-groups which involve a change of class. The statistical consequences of such misplacements depend, of course, on the frequency of the occupational title which is misplaced in class terms. Thus Kater's misplacement of foremen in mines (*Steiger*), given that these are listed under the supervisory personnel (*Angestellten*) category – part of the *Mittelstand* – in the 1925 census [102: *219*], into the 'other skilled workers' occupational sub-group of the working class has only very marginal statistical consequences [75: *6*]. Statistically more significant than Kater's misplacement of the occasional *Steiger* within the Nazi membership, at least when it comes to evaluating the social structure of the Nazi Party before 1923, is the wrong class assignment of the military by Madden (see Table 2). Soldiers, non-commissioned officers and officers were present in the Nazi Party in limited numbers in the formative phase of its development before the Munich Putsch of November 1923. Madden assigns enlisted men and non-commissioned officers into the working class and places officers into the *Mittelstand*, placements which run counter to those suggested by the official statisticians responsible for the 1933 census [88: *43*]. In the 1933 census soldiers and non-commissioned officers were included in the lower and intermediate civil servants sub-group, and officers in the higher civil servants category [102: *19*]. In their more recent work on the social background of the membership of the Nazi Party, Falter and Mühlberger follow the advice on the placement of military personnel provided by the 1933 census officials [39: *91–2*]. The fact that quite a few Nazi members in their twenties – and even some in their teens, as in the case of fifteen-year-old HJ members in the Palatinate – described themselves as merchants (*Kaufmann*) [101: *129*], whereas their age would suggest that they were not of independent status and more likely to have been commercial employees (*Handlungsgehilfen*), only distorts the percentages of these occupational sub-groups, but does not affect the overall percentage of the (lower-) middle-class component in the membership of the Nazi Movement. The same applies to the many young Nazis who listed their occupation as 'farmer', when in reality they were probably 'assisting family members', and recorded as such in the 1925 and 1933 census returns.

Although the census statisticians provide considerable guidance in both the 1925 and 1933 censuses on where to draw the boundary between the working class and the middle class, the same does not apply when it comes to differentiating between the middle class and the upper class. The economic, cultural and social elite (*Oberschicht*) in German society combined in diverse patterns wealth, income, education and prestige or esteem of occupation or rank, and in occupational terms – and here the censuses of the time do provide important clues – straddled the upper middle class and upper class. In the literature on the social elements supporting the Nazi Movement there are considerable differences in resolving the problem of identifying the 'elite social stratum', which accounted for 2 to 3 per cent of German society in the inter-war years [75: *12–13*]. While Brustein and Falter (see Table 4) dispense with an elite component in their social ranking scheme altogether, Kater (see Table 1) and Mühlberger (see Table 3) assign managers, higher civil servants, academic professionals, entrepreneurs and estate owners to the elite. Madden (see Table 2) has a more restricted 'elite' concept and only places 'capitalists, industrialists, large landowners and those with private incomes' into the elite.

One other grouping which presents methodological problems leading to diverse approaches in classification among scholars is the student category. Whereas Madden (see Table 2) places all students into the *Mittelstand*, and Brustein and Falter (see Table 4) appear to lose them under the 'without occupation' category, Kater (see Table 1) argues for their inclusion in the elite component of German society on the basis that 'upper-school and university students customarily belong to the social elite . . . because of the prestigious and well-paying professions they may look forward to after graduation' [75: *12*]. The latter assumption is questionable when applied to the Weimar period. Graduates were not immune from unemployment throughout the 1920s and were hard hit by the massive unemployment which affected Germany in the early 1930s. Nor was it inevitable that a grammar school pupil would go on to attend university, given the serious financial constraints of many middle-class parents in the 1920s. Given that Kater differentiates between engineers trained at polytechnic-type institutions, whom he assigns to the 'non-academic professionals' sub-group which forms part of the middle class in his occupational and class model, and those who attended university, whom he includes in the 'academic professionals' sub-group which forms part of the elite [75: *8*], it would seem unwise to place all students in the same category. In Mühlberger's occupational and class model (see Table 3) university students and non-university students are classified separately. University students, who had a penchant for indicating their 'university status' by giving their field of study in abbreviated form in Latin by describing themselves as *stud. phil.* or *cand. med.*, are placed by him into the upper middle class and upper class, while those who described themselves as a grammar school pupil (*Gymnasiast*) or simply as a 'student' (*Student*) are assigned to the lower and middle middle class [102: *18–19*]. In his more recent work Mühlberger has removed school pupils (*Schüler*) from the non-university students sub-group and now places them into the 'status unclear' category [39: *90–1*].

Although differences continue to exist between the occupational classification schemes and class models employed by those working on the analysis of the social characteristics of the membership and leadership of the Nazi Movement, the differences have fortunately – for comparative purposes – narrowed over time. The statistical impact arising out of the still existing differences is now relatively marginal when it comes to defining the overall class structure of the support mobilised by the Nazis. Only in Madden's scheme, given his continued placement of all artisans into the *Mittelstand*, are the working-class and middle-class percentage values significantly out of step with those produced by Kater, Mühlberger and Brustein and Falter. Once the classification schemes used in the data analyses of the 1980s and 1990s were more closely based on those to be found in the 1925 and 1933 censuses, the data values produced for the working-class, middle-class and upper-class share of the Nazi membership converged significantly. The comparatively marginal statistical differences still to be found in the literature might be further reduced if, as Andrews suggests, the data available is encoded in what he calls its 'hardest form'. He suggests that those working on the theme should use as fine a differentiation as is possible, since this would allow 'for the possibility of fitting data into different models for the purpose of comparing their validity or for juxtaposing various sub-groups'. This would, of course, markedly increase the number of social categories and occupational groups employed in tabulating data [4: *312–16*]. Andrews' suggestion of a classification model divided into seven social categories and thirty-eight occupational sub-groups does, however, raise practical difficulties when it comes to publishing the huge tables which would be generated by such a model.

There is little to suggest that the historians and political scientists who produced the first quantitative studies on the sociology of the Nazi Movement in the 1970s were guided by the massive amount of information on the social structure of the working population of Weimar Germany which is to be found in the introductory volumes to the census returns of 1925 and 1933. In both of these tens of thousands of occupational titles are listed alphabetically, with indications as to where in social space they are to be placed. Unskilled, semi-skilled and skilled workers, including dependent artisans (*Handwerker*), in the primary, secondary and tertiary sectors of the economy, were all routinely assigned to the working class by the census officials in both 1925 and 1933. The statisticians were less sure about the two categories of 'cottage industry workers' (comprising *Hausgewerbetreibende* and *Heimarbeiter*) and 'domestic employees' (*Hausangestellte*). In the 1925 census the cottage industry workers were included under 'independents', but in the 1933 census they were included in the 'workers' category. 'Domestic employees' were placed under neither the 'workers' nor 'employees' category in 1925, but counted separately, as they were again in 1933, though by then they were deemed to be partly 'blue-collar workers' and partly 'white-collar employees'. These categories have very little statistical significance overall, for 'cottage industry workers' accounted for only 0.8 per cent of the (male) blue-collar workforce in the 1920s, while the figure for (male) 'domestic employees' was a mere 0.1 per cent [103: *51*]. Of the 21,604 blue-collar workers – all but a handful of whom were male – who joined the Nazi Party between 1925 and 1933 in various regions of Germany analysed by Mühlberger, only two gave *Heimarbeiter* as their occupation [103: *66*]. Occupational titles relating to the 'cottage industry workers' and 'domestic employees' categories were hardly in evidence among the predominantly male Nazi membership, and whether one places these occupational groups under the working class or (lower) middle class has virtually no discernible impact on the overall class profile of the Nazi Movement.

As far as the identification of the working class is concerned there is one other group which provides special problems, the unskilled, semi-skilled and skilled blue-collar workers employed in the public sector. Identifying these, which is difficult – if indeed not impossible – from the sort of information contained in membership registers or on membership cards, is important in that the assertion is often made in the literature that blue-collar workers in the public sector were particularly prominent among the working-class elements to be found in the Nazi Movement [125: *27*; 126: *132*]. From the census data it is possible to identify those blue-collar workers employed in public utilities, in public transport and in the postal services. Blue-collar workers in these economic sectors accounted for just under 6 per cent of the total male workforce in 1925, but for some 80 per cent of public blue-collar workers as a whole [103: *50–1*]. Neither unskilled nor semi-skilled and skilled workers in the public sector – as far as these can be accurately identified – appear to have been of much significance in the Nazi Party membership in various regions of Germany on which we have extensive information [103: *62–3, 65–6*]. The placement of those blue-collar workers who can be identified as working in the public sector into either the working class or the lower middle class has seemingly little statistical impact.

The third problem area as far as the methodological issues raised in handling data relating to the Nazi Movement are concerned centres on the question of the representative nature of the material being evaluated. Drawing sweeping conclusions about the social base of the Nazi Movement from a small, statistically unrepresentative membership sample (such as that which was available to Abel), or on the basis of the few membership lists (such as those unearthed by Franz-Willing and by Maser), is obviously risky and methodologically flawed. Nor can data on the Nazi Party's membership relating to a short time-span be used as a basis for making pronouncements about its membership configuration over time. The breakdown of the Nazi Party's membership provided in the *Partei-Statistik* – based on only 60 per cent or so of the membership actually enrolled between the end of February 1925 and the end of January 1933 – obviously does not provide a reliable and accurate guide to the social composition of the entire party membership in this period. Similar problems surround the work on the social make-up of the membership and leadership of the Nazi Party's specialist organisations. Fischer became involved in a lively exchange of views on methodological issues when he aggregated various sources of the SA – comprising members resident in different regions of Germany and data relating to different time-periods – into a sample on the basis of which he drew conclusions about the social background of the rank-and-file storm troopers before Hitler became chancellor [10; 11; 44].

The methods employed in utilising the extensive holdings of the BDC have also given rise to questions about how far the data acquired by scholars who have gone that route is representative. Kater drew a strictly proportional sample of 18,255 Nazi members from the BDC, covering the period 1925 to 1945 [73: *476*]. However, his sample contained only 2,186 cases for the years 1925 to 1932 [73: *476*] – a period in which over a million members joined the NSDAP – 1,954 of whom joined in the period 1930 to 1932 [75: *250–1*]. This leaves a statistically insufficient sample of only 232 cases for the years 1925 to 1929. Unlike Kater's sample, which is based on membership cards selected from across the whole of the alphabet, Madden's comparatively massive BDC sample of 47,438 members who joined the party during the period 1925 to 1932 involves the combination of a systematic and a total sample [94: *124*]. He evaluated all those members whose surnames start with the letters C, D, E, I, P, R, U, V and Z. This sampling method, the representative nature of which Madden considers to be 'incontrovertible', probably skewed his results in view of the regional clustering of surnames in Germany [21: *88*]. The systematic sample organised and supervised by Brustein and Falter, the second largest of the BDC-based samples involving 42,004 cases [20: *17*; 21: *88*], is probably the nearest to a representative sample extracted from the BDC holdings to date.

Reservations have also been expressed about the representative nature of the results obtained by different scholars who have dealt with the question of the social geometry of the Nazi electorate, as well as the methodologies employed by them [94: *165–94*; 82]. The pre-war studies by Stephan [128–31] and the bulk of the post-war studies on the Nazi electorate, such as those by Bracher, Childers, Hamilton and Hänisch [16; 26; 56; 57], are invariably non-representative in nature, on the basis of which conclusions are drawn on the social characteristics of the Nazi voters as a whole. The studies by Childers and Hänisch, both published in 1983, were the first to use modern quantitative methods involving multivariate regression analysis. Childers, by excluding all counties and urban units which had 'experienced significant redistricting', restricted his analysis to 246 agrarian counties and 212 urban units, which allowed him to examine the behaviour of only just short of 50 per cent of the population entitled to vote in the *Reichstag* elections from 1924 to 1932 [26: *278*]. As he himself admitted, his 'large' or 'broad' sample was not a representative one [26: *7, 9*]. Significant errors in Childers' statistical methods, especially the high intercorrelations of the many variables used in his multivariate regression analysis, also undermine the value of his conclusions [94: *174*; 33: *384*]. Hänisch investigated all seven *Reichstag* elections in which the Nazis were involved between 1924 and 1933, and examined all 787 'stable' territorial units of the German Reich, making due allowance for territorial adjustments [57: *1*]. He did not, however, include all of these units in his multivariate regression analysis, leaving 161 'mixed rural/urban' units aside [57: *103*], thereby limiting the representative nature of his analysis by excluding some 20 per cent or so of the total electorate from his calculations [94: *178*]. The value of the first representative analysis of the Nazi electorate by Courtney Brown [19], who examined all of the 946 counties of the Weimar Republic, is limited by the fact that he dealt only with the July 1932 *Reichstag* election, used too few variables and excluded the large electoral group 'assisting family members' from his calculations [94: *180–1*]. The utility of the collaborative analysis by O'Loughlin, Flint and Anselin is similarly limited by being restricted to the *Reichstag* election of September 1930 [110].

Among the various methodological issues encountered in the analysis of the sociology of the Nazi electorate [82; 133] one needs especial reference, that of 'ecological fallacy' [26: *271–2*; 56: *500–1*]. The increasingly sophisticated cliometrics employed in modern studies on the social configuration of the Nazi electorate all rely on aggregate-level data analysis which, as Brustein puts it, 'can provide neither direct information on the political preferences among specific social strata or occupational groups nor knowledge of the specific characteristics of individual Nazi Party supporters'. He goes on to note that it cannot be assumed 'that because individuals in a particular set of geographical units with a particular pattern of social and demographic characteristics behaved in a particular way, that all people in those geographic areas who possessed most or all of the same characteristics behaved in the same fashion. This is the so-called ecological fallacy' [20: *13*]. It is the absence of any controls of the results in the form of exit polls or polls of voting intentions for the Weimar period which is a major deficit when it comes to accurately determining the voting behaviour of the different class elements in German society.

The methodological problems which surround the analyses of the sociology of the membership of the Nazi Movement and of the electorate of the Nazi Party are not always made explicit enough, and at times are even ignored by those working in the field. That should be borne in mind when the statistical material available on the social bases of Nazism in the extensive literature now at hand is evaluated. Manfred Kuechler notes that 'at times, researchers get carried away with numbers, with the fascination of seemingly precise quantitative measurement', and gives the warning that there are limits to what quantitative analysis can accomplish, especially when it comes to multivariate regression analysis [82: *30–5*].

Chapter 4

The social characteristics of the Nazi Party in its formative years, 1919–1923

In its early years the Nazi Party was primarily a south German – predominantly Bavarian – phenomenon, a peripheral movement of no significance in the national politics of the Weimar Republic. Founded by Anton Drexler and Karl Harrer in Munich on 5 January 1919, the German Workers' Party (*Deutsche Arbeiterpartei* – DAP, renamed NSDAP in February 1920) was still a tiny sect-like affair when Hitler joined it in September 1919, with a small membership which probably did not exceed the forty mark. By the time the first party census was taken in late November or early December, the membership had grown to 168, with a further 21 members joining the DAP by January 1920. In the years 1920 to 1922 the Nazi Party experienced very moderate growth and remained a very marginal, weak affair in Germany as a whole, even in its stronghold of Bavaria. The party had issued 2,000 membership cards by the end of 1920 and a further 18,000 members were enrolled in the course of 1921 and 1922. At first much of this growth was generated in Munich itself, though a number of branches were gradually established in Bavaria in 1920, the first of these being founded in Rosenheim in April. By the end of 1920 a few isolated branches had also appeared outside of Bavaria, starting with the formation of a branch in May in Stuttgart in the state of Württemberg, the emergence of the first branch north of the river Main by May at Dortmund in the Prussian province of Westphalia, and the foundation of a branch in Pforzheim in Baden in October. The expansion and development of Nazism in much of Germany, however, was seriously handicapped from late 1922 onwards, when the Nazi Party was banned in one state after another, starting with its prohibition in Prussia in November 1922. This led more often than not to the collapse of the comparatively few branches in existence in northern, eastern and central Germany, or forced the party to go underground, with isolated grouplets of Nazis living a shadowy existence in much of Germany by 1923. It was only in southern Germany that the party was free to operate unhindered.

In his review of the history and development of the Nazi Party in January 1923, Hitler asserted that the party had more members in Munich than in the rest of Germany put together. Munich retained its role in 1923 as the motor of a party that experienced further expansion primarily of its branch network and membership in Bavaria and Württemberg, growth which occurred in the emotion-laden atmosphere generated by the occupation of the Ruhr by French and Belgian troops in January 1923. The nationalist hysteria aroused by the Ruhr occupation, combined with the social and political fall-out of the hyper-inflation raging in Germany, along with the widespread resentment of the Versailles Treaty in the post-war years, conditioned the growth of radical forces both on the left and right of the political spectrum. One of the beneficiaries of the deteriorating economic and political situation in 1923 was the Nazi Party, which markedly increased its support in the course of the year, at least in southern Germany. By the time of the abortive Munich Putsch on 9 November 1923, the Nazi Party had issued 55,787 membership cards, that is, it had enrolled 55,287 individuals since its formation in January 1919, given that the Nazis had started their central party membership register with the number 500! There is no way of knowing how many of these members were still in the party by November 1923. What is known is that some 35,000 membership cards had been issued in 1923, including around 10,000 issued between 25 September and 9 November 1923, when the party was banned throughout Germany following the fiasco of its revolutionary attempt to seize power. Details on 4,786 of these 10,000 newly registered members have survived, some 68 per cent of whom were resident in the state of Bavaria. Here the party had branches numbering several thousand strong in Munich and Nuremberg, as well as sizeable branches in a number of other towns, especially in Protestant parts of Franconia in northern Bavaria, a region of major Nazi growth in 1923 [101: *52–3*].

A systematic sample of the membership of the Nazi Party from its emergence up to the time of its total national ban in November

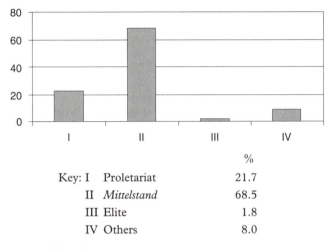

Key: I   Proletariat   21.7
II *Mittelstand*   68.5
III Elite   1.8
IV Others   8.0

Source: [88: *43*].

Figure 3   The social ranking of the membership of the Nazi Party
between 1919 and 1923 according to Madden (N: 8,144)

1923 is not feasible, given that only the fragment noted above of
the party's central membership register has survived, along with
a number of branch membership lists which provide snapshots of
the social background of Nazi supporters in various localities at
different points in time. The fragmentary nature of the data therefore dictates that longitudinal macro studies on the sociology of the
early Nazi Party can only be based on an aggregation of the diverse
sources available. The largest of these are provided by Madden
(see Figure 3), based on 8,144 members, and by Genuneit, involving 8,059 members. Madden quantified 'the information concern-
ing each individual on all the known membership lists which have
survived from those years', but is specific about only one of these,
the 2,988 members recorded in the 'Adolf Hitler's Comrades-in-
Arms' list which he found in the BDC, which registers those members who had joined the party between February 1919 and October
1921 [88: *36*]. Genuneit is even vaguer as to the exact sources which
he used, merely noting that these involve 'the membership lists of the
NSDAP from the period 1919 to 1923' [52: *35*]. The suspicion is
that both used virtually identical membership lists. Since Genuneit
is primarily concerned with the methodological issues involved
in analysing membership data, he only breaks down the membership

according to its occupational status [52: *59*], whereas Madden provides both social ranking and occupational distribution. The dominance of the membership drawn from the middle class is very striking in Madden's data, in which the working-class members form only just short of 22 per cent, some 6 per cent lower than the percentage for 'workers' to be found in Genuneit's data [52: *59*]. The difference in the working-class values is basically due to methodological preferences: the inclusion of dependent artisans by Genuneit in the working class and their placement in the *Mittelstand* by Madden. If one uses Kater's formula of automatically assigning two-thirds of the artisans to the working class, then Madden's value for the working-class element in his sample increases by 9.5 per cent to 31.2 per cent.

Neither the Madden nor the Genuneit data can be considered as representative of the social characteristics of the membership of the Nazi Party in its early years as a whole. What can be established, however, on the basis of what appears to be the complete data listing 2,548 of 'Adolf Hitler's Comrades-in-Arms', is the social profile of the individuals who had joined the party in Munich by August 1921 [29; 101: *55*]. All but 2.2 per cent of these early Nazis were resident in Munich. The breakdown of the membership indicates that in its formative phase of development the Nazi Party attracted a socially mixed following in Munich. Although the core of the membership (45 per cent) was drawn from the middle class, the party also attracted a not insignificant 24 per cent of its support from the working class, as well as 10 per cent of its strength from the Munich elite. The social status of the remainder, of which 4.1 per cent were 'wives' or 'widows', is unclear [101: *55*]. The party's heterogeneous composition mirrored the social structure of Munich's population in broad terms, though the working class was marginally under-represented among its membership [23: *94–5*].

The image of a people's party, but one with an even more pronounced 'middle-class paunch' – to use Falter's apt description [33: *372*] – also emerges from the membership lists relating to a number of branches established in various parts of (mainly south) Germany, which provide an accurate insight into their social composition at a particular point in time. In the comparatively large branches established in south Germany at Rosenheim and Mannheim by August 1922, and at Landshut and Ingolstadt by late 1923, middle-class elements provided an absolute majority of the membership, while the percentage for working-class members ranged from a low of 16.6 per cent in the 320-strong Rosenheim branch, to a high of 30 per cent in the 535-strong Ingolstadt branch [101: *55–6*]. Blue-collar workers were slightly more noticeable among the 232 members who joined the Nazi Party in Leipzig in Saxony between November 1922 and April 1923, accounting for 34.7 per cent of a membership dominated by individuals drawn from the middle class, who provided 55.6 per cent of the branch membership [104: *211–12*].

An insight into the social types which rushed towards the Nazi Party on the eve of its abortive attempt to seize power in November 1923 can be derived from the large fragment of the central membership register which has survived, which lists 4,786 of the roughly 10,000 members (the register begins with membership number 45,000 and ends with entry number 55,787, but has lengthy gaps) who joined the party between 25 September and 9 November 1923. The publication of the results of Kater's analysis of this list in 1971 marks the beginning of the relatively numerous quantitative studies on the sociology of the Nazi Party available today [70]. In his first analysis of this major piece of empirical material, Kater's very restricted definition of the German working class as comprising only unskilled workers allowed him to reach the conclusion that virtually the whole of the 4,726 new members whom he analysed were drawn from the lower middle class. The lopsided class profile (see Figure 2, Model A) of the Nazi membership which Kater's approach resulted in, one in which only 9.5 per cent were deemed 'working class', as against the 90.5 per cent considered to be 'lower middle class' (included in which were 8.5 per cent classified as 'skilled workers', 1.7 per cent listed under 'domestic workers' and 20 per cent described as 'artisans') permitted Kater strongly to underpin the prevailing 'middle-class thesis' of the time [70: *159*]. Some ten years or so later Kater reworked the bulk of the data (he reduced the number subjected to analysis to the 4,454 individuals who had provided occupational data) on the basis of a revamped occupational and class model (see Figure 2, Model B). The class profile was strikingly different to that which his original analysis had arrived at, with 35.9 per cent now assigned to the working class, 52.1 per cent to the lower-middle class, and 11.9 per cent to the elite [75: *243*].

Mühlberger's calculations based on the same source (see Figure 4), but using all of the 4,786 entries in the register, reflect a

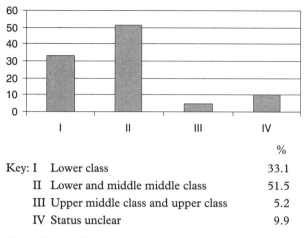

Key: I	Lower class	33.1
II	Lower and middle middle class	51.5
III	Upper middle class and upper class	5.2
IV	Status unclear	9.9

Source: [101: *63*].

Figure 4 The social ranking of individuals joining the Nazi Party between 25 September and 9 November 1923 according to Mühlberger (N: 4,786)

class profile not dissimilar to that arrived at by Kater following the revision of his class model [101: *63*]. Mühlberger goes several steps further by breaking the data down at the state (*Land*), regional and local level, which throws up a number of interesting features which 'macro' analyses of the data cannot reveal [101: *61–72*]. Although only 32.3 per cent of the new members involved in the surge towards the Nazi Party in late 1923 came from outside of Bavaria, and indeed only a mere 24.2 per cent from outside of southern Germany, the data do suggest that the Nazis – despite the ban on their party in the bulk of the German states – were in the process of establishing a toehold in many parts of northern, central and eastern Germany. Admittedly, the numbers recruited north of the Main pale into insignificance when measured by the 3,241 individuals who joined the party in Bavaria alone. The *Mittelstand* furnished the bulk of the individuals recruited by the Nazis outside of Bavaria, providing as it did the majority of new members in all of the states on which there is evidence. Recruits drawn from the working class were relatively few, though workers did provide around one third of the new membership in the states of Saxony (32.9 per cent) and Thuringia

(31.2 per cent), in the Prussian provinces of Silesia (39.2 per cent) and Westphalia (32.1 per cent), and in the electoral district of Saxony-Anhalt (32.6 per cent). Well over 1,000 (primarily skilled) blue-collar workers also joined the party in Bavaria, where they accounted for 36.3 per cent of the 3,241 new recruits [101: *62–3*].

At the micro level the social background of the new members mobilised by the Nazi Party in late 1923 shows quite striking variations. At the branch level the *Mittelstand* element did not invariably marginalise working-class types among the party joiners. In a number of south German towns which experienced significant recruitment in the six weeks or so before the Munich Putsch, workers formed the absolute majority of the new intake in a number of branches, as in Vilsbiburg (59 per cent), Starnberg (58.3 per cent), Augsburg (55.9 per cent), Pappenheim (54 per cent) and Memmingen (51.3 per cent), and provided a relative majority in Günzburg, Hof, Kulmbach and Nuremberg [101: *64–8*]. The quite diverse social mix among the recruits at the branch level is difficult to fit into a 'middle-class thesis'.

A strong middle-class presence is undoubtedly evident in the membership of the Nazi Party in its early years of development as far as the available data are concerned. It is unlikely that new data will be found which will significantly alter the current picture that we have of the social base of Nazism before November 1923. The Nazis recruited disproportionately from the *Mittelstand* in the years following the formation of their party in January 1919. But they were also able to secure significant support both from the working class and from the elite, giving the party a heterogeneous social base. It is the infinite variety in the mix of the social and occupational groups encountered at the branch level which makes it difficult to categorise the Nazi Party specifically as a middle-class party, even in its formative phase of development. The rag-bag of ideas peddled by the Nazis attracted a socially mixed following right from the start, ranging from aristocratic landowners and factory directors at the top of the social scale to day labourers and casual workers at the bottom.

Chapter 5

The social characteristics of the membership and leadership of the Nazi Party, 1925–1933

After 9 November 1923 the Nazi Party was banned for the first time throughout Germany, though in Thuringia the ban lasted only briefly and was lifted as early as 3 March 1924. One option not open to Hitler, therefore, on his release on 20 December 1924 from Landsberg prison, where he had served less than a year of a five-year sentence for treason imposed on him in the spring of 1924, was to re-found the Nazi Party. Since the general consensus in Bavaria, as in Germany in general, was that the Nazis were a spent force and unlikely to cause any problems if they were allowed to be politically active again, the Bavarian government lifted the ban on the Nazi Party on 16 February 1925, a step which the various other *Länder* governments rapidly followed. That development opened the door for Hitler to re-found the Nazi Party on 27 February 1925.

The environment in which the re-launched Nazi Party operated after February 1925 was one of relative calm in comparison with the turbulence the Weimar state had gone through in the immediate post-war years and the disaster yet to come at the end of the decade in the shape of the Great Depression, when mass unemployment, social stress and political chaos combined to strangle German democracy. After comparatively rapid growth in 1925, at the end of which the Nazis had enrolled around 27,000 members, the party settled down to steady, if unspectacular, expansion. By the end of 1928 the Nazi Party had issued its 100,000th membership card and was in the process of shedding its Bavarian image and acquiring a national profile. In 1929 the move towards the party accelerated, and 70,000 new membership cards were issued during the year. The 'take-off' phase of the party occurred in 1930. It coincided with a marked deepening of the agrarian and industrial crises which had beset Germany in the late 1920s, plunging the Weimar Republic into a sustained political crisis from the spring of 1930. The democratic process was virtually frozen as a consequence, with a succession of presidential governments culminating in the final destruction of the Republic's pluralist parliamentary democracy with the establishment and consolidation of the so-called 'National Government' under the chancellorship of Hitler in the spring and summer of 1933. As unemployment rose to astronomic levels after 1930, to the point at which by 1932 almost 30 per cent of the working population were without work, radicals of the left and right latched on to – and exploited – the deprivation, anxiety and anger of large sections of German society.

That the Nazis benefited from the crisis more than any other party opposed to Weimar democracy is well known. After the Nazi electoral breakthrough in the *Reichstag* election of September 1930, in which the Nazi Party secured 18.3 per cent of the vote as against the 2.6 per cent it had recorded in the *Reichstag* election of May 1928, a veritable stampede towards the party took place as large numbers of *Septemberlinge*, as established Nazis disparagingly dubbed the newcomers, joined the party. By the end of 1930 the 400,000th membership card had been issued. The ominous surge towards the Nazi Party in 1930 was sustained in 1931 and 1932, when a further 100,000 membership cards were issued on average at three-monthly intervals. By the time Hitler became chancellor at the end of January 1933, the party had handed out a total of 1,435,530 membership cards. These figures hide, however, the volatility of the Nazi Party's membership. By the time the Nazis subjected their followers to a census in the course of 1934, only just short of 850,000 of the 1.4 million members who had been enrolled before 30 January 1933 were still in the party. Since it is unlikely that any significant number of these would have left the party after Hitler was appointed chancellor, when party membership took on a new meaning and became rapidly and increasingly important, it would seem that the Nazi Party lost around 40 per cent of those who had joined it at some stage before the end of January 1933.

For the period February 1925 to January 1933 there are three sets of data available on the social structure of the Nazi Party at the macro level, indeed four, if one includes the *Partei-Statistik* (see Figure 1) produced by the Nazis themselves. The three data sets

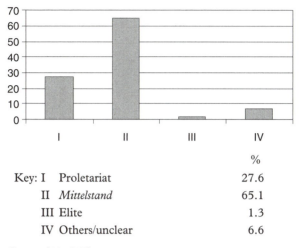

Key: I   Proletariat   27.6
     II *Mittelstand*   65.1
     III Elite   1.3
     IV Others/unclear   6.6

Source: [91: *273*].

Figure 5   The social ranking of individuals joining the Nazi Party between 1925 and 1933 according to Madden (N: 47,438)

are all based on samples drawn from the BDC, and involve a small unrepresentative sample taken by Kater (see Figure 2, Model B), and two large samples, that by Madden (see Figure 5) and that by Brustein and Falter (see Figure 6). The values arrived at by Kater and by Brustein and Falter are broadly in line, though it has to be borne in mind that they employ class and occupational models (see Tables 1 and 4) which show slight variations. Moreover, Kater based his calculations only on those Nazi members who were part of the working population, and left aside those individuals who were retired or without an occupation, such as pensioners, housewives and widows, so that strictly speaking like is not being compared with like. But the values for the working-class component among the newcomers to the Nazi Party in the two sets of data are virtually identical, and those for middle-class recruits only marginally higher in Kater's data. It is only Madden's breakdown of the social ranking of individuals joining the Nazi Party in these years which is very much out of step with those arrived at by Kater and by Brustein and Falter. It is ironic that Madden, a staunch advocate of the 'people's party thesis', began to publish statistical evidence in the 1980s in which the *Mittelstand* loomed very large, while in

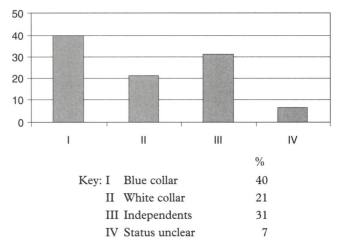

Key: I   Blue collar   40
II   White collar   21
III   Independents   31
IV   Status unclear   7

Source: [21: *92*].

Figure 6   The occupational status of individuals joining the Nazi Party between 1925 and 1932 according to Brustein and Falter (N: 39,812)

the same decade Kater began to publish data which seriously undermined the position he had taken in the 1970s as the major champion of the 'lower-middle-class thesis' of Nazism. The discrepancies between Madden's class values and those of Kater and of Brustein and Falter are primarily due to Madden's placement of all artisans into the middle class, the consequence of which significantly reduces the working-class content within the ranks of the Nazi Party, and, conversely, inflates its middle-class component. Included in Madden's *Mittelstand* value of 65.1 per cent is a sizeable artisan occupational sub-group accounting for 18.5 per cent of the membership, the bulk of which undoubtedly involved dependent artisans, who should be included in the working class. When Kater's method of automatically assigning 63.4 per cent of all artisans to the working class is used, the percentage of the membership drawn by the Nazi Party from the working class in the period February 1925 to January 1933 in Madden's sample increases to 39 per cent, while that for the *Mittelstand* is reduced to 53 per cent. If one compares the 'amended' Madden data set with those of Kater and

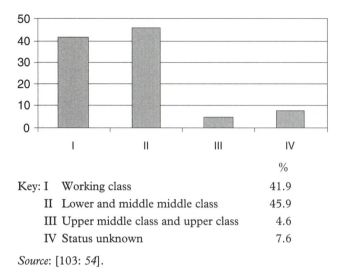

Key: I   Working class   41.9
     II   Lower and middle middle class   45.9
     III Upper middle class and upper class   4.6
     IV   Status unknown   7.6

Source: [103: *54*].

Figure 7   The social ranking of individuals in the Nazi Party between 1925 and 1932 according to Mühlberger (N: 52,579)

of Brustein and Falter, the values arrived at for the working class and for the middle class are not overly dissimilar.

Data on the social make-up of the Nazi Party's membership analysed by Mühlberger (see Figure 7) also provides values which are in line with the results obtained from the BDC material sampled by Kater, Madden (in its amended form) and Brustein and Falter. Mühlberger's data, however, cannot be viewed as representative for the Nazi Party as a whole since it is not a systematic sample. His results are based on the aggregation of extensive Nazi membership records relating to six regions of Germany, including two large sets of data recording all of the newly enrolled members in *Gau* Hesse-Nassau-South for the period 1929 to 30 January 1933, and for *Gau* Württemberg for the years 1928 to 1930 [103: *53–4*]. What is particularly interesting about the party's recruitment patterns in *Gaue* Württemberg-Hohenzollern and Hesse-Nassau-South is that they show that the percentage levels for workers entering the party in these *Gaue* were much greater than those claimed for these regions in the *Partei-Statistik* of 1935. For in *Gau* Württemberg-Hohenzollern workers provided 42.5 per cent of the newly enrolled

members (N: 4,117) between 1928 and 1930 [102: *83*], whereas
in the *Partei-Statistik* the Nazis claimed that in this *Gau* workers
made up only 29.2 per cent of its membership (N: 2,751) before
14 September 1930 [113: *146*]. In the case of *Gau* Hesse-Nassau-
South, workers accounted for 38.1 per cent of the membership
recruited between the beginning of 1929 and 14 September 1930
[102: *122*], whereas in the *Partei-Statistik* workers provided only
29 per cent of the *Gau* membership enrolled between 1925 and 14
September 1930 [113: *146*]. Making due allowance for the differences in the respective classification schemes used, and bearing in
mind the different time-spans to which these sets of membership
data apply, it does seem that workers were entering the party in both
Gaue at a much higher rate than the *Gau* census returns of 1935 in-
dicate. The data suggests that workers were also much more likely
to leave the party over time than members drawn from the middle class or elite. This is the factor which most likely accounts for
the differences in the values given for 'workers' in the three BDC
data sets, which average out at around the 41 per cent mark for
the 1925 to 1933 period, and that of 31.5 per cent to be found in
the *Partei-Statistik*. The discrepancy between the lower figure in the
Partei-Statistik for workers in the party before 30 January 1933 and
the higher values to be found in the data sets produced by historians
analysing the BDC holdings seems to suggest that the Nazis were
not, as has often been claimed, massaging the membership census
returns to support their claim to be an authentic *Volkspartei*.

Parallel to the publication of the macro data sets on the social profile of the Nazi membership came a series of micro studies analysing
the composition of the membership of the Nazi Party at the regional
and local level. A pioneering study by Lawrence Stokes focussed on
a list of 469 members belonging to the Nazi Party branch established
in the small town of Eutin in north Germany [132]. Stokes' analysis
revealed that the 'proletarian' element in the branch (composed of
unskilled, semi-skilled and skilled workers, domestic workers and
dependent artisans), which formed 36.5 per cent of the membership, was over-represented in comparison with the size of the working class in Eutin, given at 25 per cent. In his major study on the
membership and leadership of the Nazi Party, Kater provides a
number of branch breakdowns which showed not only the variable
social configuration of Nazi branches in different parts of Germany

at different times, but also the high working-class percentages to be found in some branches [75: *246–7, 250*]. In a study on the social profile of the Nazi Party in the Border Province Posen-West Prussia, Mühlberger demonstrated that even in a predominantly agrarian region the NSDAP was able to attract a socially mixed following, including a significant level of working-class support. The analysis also revealed the often quite different social configuration of branch membership in a region in which such factors as economic structure, level of urbanisation, the religious conviction and social structure of the population were virtually constant [100]. The infinite variability of the social background of the membership mobilised by the Nazi Party at the local level also emerges as a central feature of Mühlberger's examination of the party in different regions of Germany [102]. Whereas the middle class dominated twenty-six of the sixty party branches recruiting in *Gau* Hesse-Nassau-South between 1928 and 1931, including the very large branches at Frankfurt-am-Main (N: 3,979) and Wiesbaden (N: 1,607), workers provided the single largest social grouping among the party newcomers in thirty-four small and medium-sized branches, with an absolute majority in twenty-seven of them [102: *100–15*]. In *Gau* Württemberg-Hohenzollern the pattern was very similar, with workers providing the majority of new members in twenty-seven of the forty-three branches recruiting between 1928 and 1930, and an absolute majority in twenty-one of them. The sizeable Stuttgart branch, however, drew 59 per cent of its 688 new members from the *Mittelstand*, while in the university town of Tübingen it was university students (32.4 per cent) who provided more new members than either the working class (30.4 per cent) or the middle class (26.8 per cent) [102: *66–77*]. Other areas on which there is detailed information on the social configuration of membership of the Nazi Party at the branch level show similar patterns [39; 104].

   On the eve of its acquisition of power, the Nazi Party represented a microcosm of German society in terms of the social make-up of its membership. Within its ranks were people drawn from all walks of life. In the course of its rapid expansion from the late 1920s, the party had penetrated into all corners of Germany and mobilised support from all 'Christian' persuasions, from all classes, irrespective of whether these were resident in isolated rural areas, or in heavily industrialised regions, or in urban sprawls. Although the membership of the Nazi Party did not reflect the class structure of German society perfectly in that the working class was under-represented – and the middle class over-represented – within it, it did in the course of the early 1930s lose to some extent the pro-nounced 'middle-class paunch' which it had exhibited in its for-mative years. The membership of the party was characterised by a remarkably heterogeneous structure, and the infinite variability of the social components which constituted the Nazi Party's rank-and-file at the branch level is particularly striking.

In sharp contrast to the social diversity of its ordinary member-ship, the Nazi Party's cadre was made up overwhelmingly of mem-bers drawn from the *Mittelstand* and from the elite. 'The typical Nazi leader', to quote Ronald Rogowski, 'was . . . a secure, rather successful professional, official or businessman with a history of considerable upward mobility before he had joined the movement' [117: *402*]. The evidence available on the party's functionary corps does show a fairly consistent pattern before 1933 [28; 53; 75; 101; 115; 117]. At the lower and intermediary level of the party's or-ganisational hierarchy in the *Gaue*, individuals with a middle-class background occupied the majority of the posts. In *Gau* Baden over 80 per cent of the branch and district leaders were middle class in background in the late 1920s [101: *98*]. Not one of the thirteen district leaders of *Gau* Munich-Upper Bavaria in June 1931 had working-class origins [101: *100*]. In the Nazi functionary corps in Middle and Upper Franconia in the years 1930 to 1933 only one of the seventeen branch and district leaders was a worker, whereas fourteen came from the middle class and two from the elite [101: *98*]. Three-quarters of the branch leaders in the governmental dis-trict of Kassel in Hesse in 1930, and three-quarters of the branch leaders in the Lüneburg region in 1931 were also drawn from the lower middle class [75: *256*]. Even in *Gau* Greater Berlin in the latter half of the 1920s, a period in which *Gauleiter* Goebbels was mak-ing strenuous efforts to recruit more workers into the party, almost three-quarters of the functionary corps was drawn from the *Mittel-stand* [101: *98*]. An exception to this general pattern is provided by the Ruhr region, where the dominance of the working class among the working population and its greater presence within the rank-and-file of the party [102: *26–49*] does appear to have had some

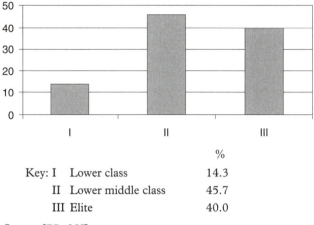

Key: I   Lower class   14.3
    II Lower middle class   45.7
    III Elite   40.0

Source: [75: *257*].

Figure 8   The social ranking of the *Gauleiter* corps in 1933 according to Kater (N: 35)

influence upon the social composition of the local leadership corps. According to data relating to the Western Ruhr, 45 per cent of the twenty branch functionaries on whom there is evidence for 1925 and 1926 were workers, and half of the twenty-two branch leaders in district Essen came from the working class in 1929 [101: *98–9*]. The attitude of the *Gauleiter* in the region was probably the factor leading to the advancement of 'workers' to a position of authority within the party, at least at the branch level. *Gauleiter* Josef Wagner of Westphalia certainly took the class factor into consideration when appointing local and district leaders, ensuring that these were drawn from the working class in the industrialised areas within his *Gau* [101: *97*]. However, when it came to the top jobs in the *Gau* administration, both Wagner, as well as Terboven in the adjacent district Essen, depended – like most *Gauleiter* – on the administrative skills and expertise of individuals drawn from the *Mittelstand* and from the elite. In the *Gauleiter* corps (see Figure 8) – the 'middle management' of the party as it were – the presence of individuals drawn from the *Mittelstand* is less in evidence due to the massive over-representation of elite elements. Individuals with a working-class background, such as the agricultural labourer Hildebrand, who became *Gauleiter* of Mecklenburg following the re-formation of the

Nazi Party in 1925, were very much the exception in the *Gauleiter* corps.

In the scramble for power within the party at the *Gau* level and above, individuals from the middle class and the elite – more often than not with a university education – were much more successful in acquiring leadership positions than those with a working-class background. The need for people of talent to control and direct the organisation and propaganda arm of the party gave the better-educated party members significant advantages in the acquisition of party posts which required expertise and bureaucratic skills. The strength of the *Mittelstand* and of the elite within the Nazi Party cadre at *Gau* level and above is not that surprising. In the Weimar period even working-class organisations developed leadership cadres based on individuals drawn from the middle class, for functional reasons. For as Kater observes, the Nazi functionary corps

> was closely related to the complex system of administrative tasks to be performed by the party hierarchy: the higher the degree of skill required, the more qualified and sophisticated were the administrative personnel. The NSDAP thus appears to have been ruled by the same laws of rationality that governed other institutions, corporations, and even other political parties in the Weimar Republic.
>
> [75: *177*]

Not surprising either is that the dominance of the middle and upper classes in the party cadre is also reflected in the share-out of the spoils accruing from the growth in the electoral support of the Nazi Party in the late 1920s and early 1930s at the local, regional and national level. It was only at the town and district council level that the working-class members in the party had a chance of being placed highly enough on the party slate to have a good chance of being elected. In 1933 workers provided a quarter of the 4,404 local councillors analysed by Kater [75: *257*]. But in the more prestigious *Landtag* elections, working-class candidates were generally squeezed out by individuals drawn from the middle class and the elite. The commentary in the *Völkischer Beobachter* on the results of the elections to the Hamburg Senate in September 1931, which emphasised the 'picture of our people's community (*Volksgemeinschaft*) unifying all occupations and classes', represents the party's disingenuous attempt to cover up the comparatively

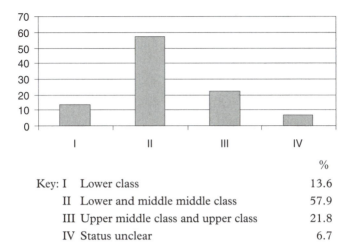

Key: I   Lower class   13.6

II Lower and middle middle class   57.9

III Upper middle class and upper class   21.8

IV Status unclear   6.7

Source: [101: *106*].

Figure 9   The social ranking of Nazi candidates in the *Reichstag* election of July 1932 according to Mühlberger (N: 838)

low level of representation of workers (eleven out of forty-three deputies) among the Nazi faction [101: *103–4*]. In Bavaria such a propaganda line was hardly feasible since there was only one skilled worker among the forty-four Nazi deputies elected to the Bavarian *Landtag* in April 1932, whereas individuals pursuing middle-class occupations made up almost three-quarters of those elected on the Nazi ticket [101: *104*]. A virtually identical situation existed in the adjacent *Land* Thuringia, where two workers figured among the twenty-six Nazi deputies elected to the *Landtag* in July 1932 [101: *103–4*]. Workers were even rarer among the candidates and grow-ing number of Nazi members elected to the *Reichstag* in the early 1930s, as reflected in the social background of the candidates who stood for office (see Figure 9), and those who were elected in what turned out to be the Nazi landslide of July 1932 (see Figure 10). The very limited success of working-class Nazis in acquiring the advantages and privileges accruing to MPs is a feature throughout the period 1928 to 1933 [101: *106–7*]. For in spite of constant at-tacks by the Nazis on the parliamentary 'system', there was intense competition among Nazi Party functionaries at all levels to be nom-inated as a *Reichstag* candidate. A 'good name', which could give

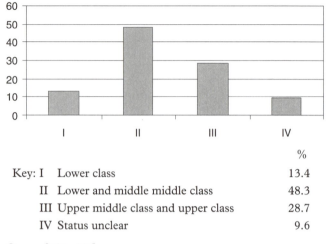

%

Key: I   Lower class   13.4
     II   Lower and middle middle class   48.3
     III Upper middle class and upper class   28.7
     IV   Status unclear   9.6

Source: [101: *106*].

Figure 10   The social ranking of Nazi deputies elected to the *Reichstag* in July 1932 according to Mühlberger (N: 230)

a degree of 'respectability' to the party, seems to have been useful for getting on to the Nazi list of *Reichstag* candidates. Preference also appears to have been given to those Nazis who already held a post of some status within the party or within one of its numerous specialist organisations [101: *109*].

In the 'scramble for posts' (*Pöstchenjägerei*) within the party, which began in earnest from the late 1920s when the party began to make some impact in a number of *Landtag* elections and emerged as a serious contender for power, Nazis with a *Mittelstand* or elite background did extremely well in securing the commanding heights of the party. The social background of the higher party functionaries and of the party's candidates and elected representatives at the *Landtag* and *Reichstag* level therefore did not bear much resemblance to the social structure of the party's ordinary membership long before the Third Reich was established.

Chapter 6

The social characteristics of the membership and leadership of Nazi specialist organisations

Beyond the framework of the Nazi Party itself, the Nazis developed a number of specialist organisations from the early 1920s onwards. These ultimately played an important role in facilitating the party's rise to power by mobilising specific gender, age, occupational and professional groups. By 1930 there were quite a number of specialist organisations officially recognised by Hitler as part of the Nazi Movement, of which all but the SA and SS had been created by the private initiative of Nazi activists, including a number of occupation-orientated organisations for teachers, lawyers and doctors. One other organisation especially important in furthering the growth of Nazism was added on 1 January 1931, when the quasi-trade union movement, the NSBO, which could trace its roots back to a number of factory cells formed in the latter half of the 1920s by Nazi activists in Berlin and elsewhere, was officially recognised by the party and integrated into the structure of the Nazi Movement. Because not all of the members enrolled in the specialist organisations – especially those active in the SA and the NSBO – were automatically members of the Nazi Party also, the various specialist organisations were important in generating support for Nazism from diverse class elements in German society whose social values and economic interests they specifically targeted through the nature of their appeal and recruitment strategy.

As in the case of the Nazi Party itself, it was only from the 1970s onwards that the social characteristics of a number of Nazi specialist organisations were examined on the basis of empirical evidence. The main focus of attention initially fell on the quasi-military SA, a party-initiated formation which could trace its origins back to 1921. It was a small affair at first, with a membership of around

1,000 by the end of 1922, which more than doubled by the time of the 'Munich Putsch' of November 1923. At that point it was – along with the NSDAP – banned throughout Germany. Following the re-formation of the Nazi Party in February 1925, the SA re-emerged also. It grew slowly in the latter half of the 1920s, reaching a total strength of some 30,000 men by August 1929 and around 60,000 men by November 1930 [43: *5*]. The explosive growth of the SA occurred in 1931 and 1932, years which saw its rapid development into a mass organisation, paralleling the expansion of the Nazi Party in these years. By January 1932 the membership of the SA had risen to 290,941, which increased further to 445,279 by August 1932. Thereafter the SA experienced a marginal reduction in its size, and by the time Hitler became chancellor it had probably around 425,000 members. Hitler's appointment to head a 'National Government' generated an explosion in the membership of the SA, which reached the 2 million mark by the summer of 1933 [43: *6*]. Unlike the NSDAP itself, the SA and the other Nazi specialist organisations were not subjected to a ban on further recruitment in the course of 1933.

The first significant analysis of the social characteristics of the membership and leadership of the SA was provided by Eric Reiche, whose doctoral thesis of 1972 – published in 1986 – dealt with the history of the SA in Nuremberg [116]. Reiche's micro study was based on the compilation of social data relating to 358 of the 12,000 or so SA members who had joined the organisation in the city between 1922 and mid-1934. This sample, probably unrepresentative of the Nuremberg SA as a whole, suggests that its ordinary membership had, in occupational and social terms, a broad class base. It showed that of the 137 rank-and-file members active in the Nuremberg SA in the period 1925 to 1932, those recruited from the working class, at 46 per cent, marginally outnumbered those drawn from the middle class, at 44.6 per cent [116: *143*]. On the basis of his case-study Reiche wisely refrained from reaching any sweeping conclusions about the sociology of the SA in Germany as a whole, but his results, especially the relatively high working-class content among his sample, gave food for thought. A few years later Peter Merkl, in his first re-working of the autobiographical accounts of individuals who had joined the Nazi Party by 1 January 1933 compiled by Theodore Abel in 1934, which included data on 337 SA members – of whom 39 were also in the SS, and 181 in leadership positions – also pointed to the broad social base of the SA elements contained in the Abel material, of which 42 per cent were of 'blue-collar workers' status [96: *595*]. In his second re-working of the Abel data which appeared a few years later, blue-collar workers (defined as 'unskilled' and 'skilled' workers) still accounted for 38.5 per cent of the 'Abel SA' [97: *99*].

A quite different picture of the social characteristics of the SA was presented in a number of articles published by Michael Kater in the 1970s, a period when he was still using the very narrow definition of the occupational groups comprising the working class which characterised all of his early work on the sociology of the Nazi Movement [71; 72]. On the basis of fragmentary material supplied to him by Conan Fischer, which comprised a number of membership records relating to SA members resident in rural Bavaria, Munich and Frankfurt-am-Main, as well as SA activists who had been arrested following brawls with political opponents in various localities in Germany, Kater argued that the SA was essentially a petit-bourgeois phenomenon, its membership – according to his odd classification scheme – being 'about 70 to 80 per cent lower middle class' before 1933 [71: *370*; 72: *801*]. In the late 1970s Fischer evaluated virtually the same material. Fischer, who used a more re-alistic class and occupational model, one in which skilled workers and dependent artisans were included in the working class, came to radically different conclusions to those reached by Kater. According to Fischer's analysis, 63.4 per cent of his sample of 1,184 SA members enrolled between 1929 and 30 January 1933 were unskilled, semi-skilled and skilled workers. In the period 31 January 1933 to 30 June 1934 the number of workers in the SA increased even further, accounting for 69.9 per cent of the 3,812 SA members on which Fischer based his calculations [41: *140*]. Fischer basically turned the social profile of the SA as suggested by Kater on its head. According to Fischer the SA was 'an activist movement which won sizeable numbers of workers for the Nationalist cause' [41: *152*]. Fischer's view of the social basis of the SA membership was supported by data published by Lawrence Stokes [132]. He analysed the occupational background of fifty-four SA members who had joined the SA in Eutin by 1929 in his micro study of the social make-up of the Nazi Party in the town. Stokes pointed to the 'proletarian' nature of the

Eutin SA, and came to the conclusion that 'in all likelihood, hardly more than half a dozen Eutin SA members enjoyed a middle-class existence' [132: *27–8*].

Fischer's essay sparked off a lively exchange revolving around methodological issues with Richard Bessel and Mathilde Jamin, both then engaged on researching different aspects of the SA. In a joint article they suggested that a number of methodological flaws undermined Fischer's work, queried the nature of the sources which he had used and cast doubts on his conclusion that the SA was strongly working class in terms of its rank-and-file membership [10]. Interestingly, however, one piece of evidence advanced by Bessel and Jamin, a police summary of the social background of 1,824 SA members resident in Berlin in February 1931, pointed in the same direction as Fischer's data, with unskilled and skilled workers accounting for 14 and 40 per cent respectively [10: *113*].

In the early 1980s Fischer, Bessel and Jamin all published the results of their research on the SA, studies which enhanced existing knowledge of that organisation in a quantitative and qualitative sense. Fischer took on board aspects of the criticism levelled against him on methodological grounds. Although he still presented his heterogeneous data in the form of aggregated large 'samples', he now produced a more differentiated breakdown of the data and placed the SA formations he was analysing into their local context. This approach highlighted the fact that unskilled and skilled workers provided the absolute majority of members in virtually all of the many individual SA units on which his data was based [43: *25–9*].

Richard Bessel, however, in his study of the SA in the predominantly rural regions of Eastern Germany, queried Fischer's conclusion that the SA was primarily a working-class outfit as far as the rank-and-file was concerned. Bessel cited statistics on the SA in East Germany put together by the police authorities in the early 1930s, data in which working-class members were less prominent. According to the police report on the SA in East Prussia for June 1931, blue-collar workers, comprising the categories of agricultural workers, industrial workers, artisans (their youth suggests that these were virtually all dependent) and apprentices, accounted for 40.5 per cent of the 4,450 SA members recruited in the governmental region of Königsberg, and for 41 per cent of the 2,144 SA members active in the governmental region of Allenstein. In data relating to the membership of the SA in Silesia for August 1930, the figure for the membership drawn from the working class was marginally higher at 45 per cent. In all three data sets it was the category 'artisans and artisans' apprentices' which accounted for between 60 and 70 per cent of the working-class element. The largest individual category within the membership, however, was that comprising 'farmers, young farmers and agricultural supervisors', who provided 34.6 per cent of the SA membership in Silesia, 35 per cent in the governmental region of Königsberg and 44.9 per cent in the governmental district of Allenstein [9: *36–7*].

Following the veritable rash of publications on the social make-up of the membership of the SA from the mid-1970s to the early 1980s, there was a brief lull. Further evidence on this question was advanced in 1987 by Mühlberger, which involved SA members recruited in Munich before the November Putsch of 1923, along with an analysis of 1,539 members of the SA resident in numerous small towns and villages scattered throughout Bavaria in early April 1932 [101: *115–22*]. The latter data demonstrated a consistent pattern of a high working-class presence within the ranks of the SA in all regions of Bavaria, ranging from 49.2 per cent in the Palatinate to 66.6 per cent in Upper Bavaria, averaging out at 61.1 per cent for Bavaria as a whole [101: *119–20*]. The structure of the SA in predominantly small-town, rural areas of Bavaria in the spring of 1932 was in marked contrast to that of the SA in rural East Prussia in 1931 as summarised in the police records which Bessel had discovered. Additional material published by Mühlberger in the early 1990s gave further strong support to Fischer's argument that the SA was predominantly working class in terms of its rank-and-file membership. In data relating to SA units recruited in the states of Bavaria and Württemberg, and in the Prussian provinces of Hesse-Nassau, Hanover and Westphalia, agricultural workers, unskilled, semi-skilled and skilled workers, as well as craftsmen, dominated the social make-up of units of 'ordinary' SA, of SA-Motor and SA-Rider corps, as well as of SA probationers and SA reservists, and confirmed Fischer's contention that the SA's rank-and-file was predominantly lower class [102: *168–71*].

The most comprehensive data set available on the SA's social composition to date is summarised in Figure 11. It combines the bulk of the data previously published by Fischer and Mühlberger

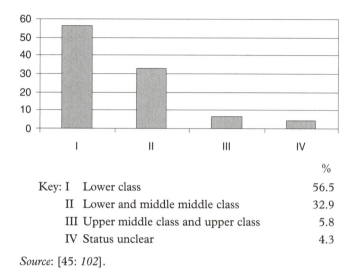

Key: I   Lower class   56.5
     II Lower and middle middle class   32.9
     III Upper middle class and upper class   5.8
     IV Status unclear   4.3

Source: [45: *102*].

Figure 11   The social ranking of the membership of the SA enrolled between 1925 and 30 January 1933 according to Fischer and Mühlberger (N: 2,643)

with additional unpublished material. The extensive source base upon which the calculations rest involves a useful mix of storm troopers resident in all regions of Germany, recruited in both rural and urban settings, in agrarian and industrial environments, and in predominantly Catholic and Protestant areas. Although even this diverse data cannot lay claim to be a representative sample on which to base an evaluation of the social profile of the SA as a whole, the aggregation of the numerous SA units on which it rests does provide the most reliable and extensive information available to date on the social pattern of the SA's membership during the Weimar Republic. The social profile the data reveals is unlikely to be significantly altered by further information on the membership of the SA yet to be unearthed in the archives. All the existing evidence points to the fact that the rank-and-file SA membership was predominantly working class in occupational and social terms before Hitler became chancellor. It does seem that the organisation was significantly more 'proletarian' than the membership of the Nazi Party itself and critical – given that over half of the storm troopers were under twenty-five years old and around 80 per cent under thirty years of age before 30 January 1933 – in mobilising significant working-class support for Nazism from the younger age cohorts of German society [43: *49*; 93].

Analysis of the class configuration of the rank-and-file members of the many other Nazi specialist organisations in existence by 1933 is at present still either lacking or in its infancy. There is limited data available on the sociology of the membership of the Hitler Youth which suggests that it had a social profile very similar to that of the SA. Relatively small in comparison with the SA, with a membership strength of around 13,000 by the end of 1929 and just over 55,000 by the end of January 1933, it appears to have drawn even more support from working-class youth during the Weimar period than the SA. Peter Stachura, on the basis of a variety of regional membership figures compiled by the HJ itself, in which the percentage for manual workers in the organisation in 1930 ranged from a low of 55 per cent in *Gau* Rhineland to a high of 77 per cent in *Gau* South Bavaria, reached the conclusion that the membership of the youth wing of the Nazi Movement was predominantly working class [124: *58–9*]. The high incidence of working-class membership in the HJ does not appear to have been a universal feature of the organisation, for in a report on the social basis of the membership of the HJ by the propaganda section of the Nazi Party in *Gau* South-Hanover-Brunswick in February 1931, workers made up only 37 per cent of the 1,200 individuals who had joined the youth wing of the Nazi Party in the region [102: *257*]. Stachura's assessment of the working-class nature of the HJ is, however, confirmed by the only extensive, detailed archival data on the membership of the HJ that has come to light to date, which was discovered and analysed by Mühlberger and which relates to the Palatinate [101: *109–14*]. At the time of the ban placed on all of the uniformed specialist organisations of the Nazi Party in April 1932, the complete register of 2,053 youths who had joined the HJ in numerous towns and villages throughout the Rhenish Palatinate between 1928 and April 1932 fell into the hands of the police. Blue-collar workers provided 57.4 per cent of those recruited by the HJ in this region in these years [101: *110*]. The HJ membership of a number of branches was solidly working class. In those established in Grünstadt, Landstuhl and Pirmasens, working-class youth provided over 80 per cent of the membership, and in the branch situated in Langmeil 100 per cent

[101: *112–13*]. While factory workers alone accounted for 50 per cent of the membership in Miesenbach, in a number of other small branches established in the rural backwaters of the province, such as Zeitkam, Wachenheim, Morschheim and St Julian, farmers' sons provided over 50 per cent of the membership, and 64.7 per cent in the case of Geiselberg [101: *113*]. According to the police report commenting on the membership records, the great bulk of the 1,101 members noted as having reached the age of eighteen were stated as having become members of the NSDAP, or of the SA, or of the SS [101: *114*].

Little light as yet has been thrown on the social characteristics of the rank-and-file membership of the SS. Along with the SA, from which it recruited the bulk of its members before 1933, the SS was one of the oldest Nazi specialist organisations by the time of the Nazi seizure of power. Following its emergence in 1925, the SS grew only very slowly in the shadow of the SA, its total strength reaching the 1,000 mark by the end of 1928, a figure which doubled by the end of 1929, and increased further to 2,727 by the end of 1930. According to statistics provided by the Nazis themselves (and these include a small number of Austrian SS members), it was only two years after Hitler had appointed Himmler to head the SS that the organisation began to grow in size, reaching a strength of 14,964 by the end of 1931, which increased to just over 52,000 by the end of 1932. A membership spurt in 1933 after Hitler became chancellor swelled its ranks to almost 210,000 by the end of the year [102: *182*].

Early attempts to grapple with the problem of the sociology of the SS undoubtedly suffered from a lack of source material and could do little more than provide impressionistic overviews of no real value [112]. In his review of the existing literature on the SS in the early 1960s, Robert Koehl, commenting on the social background of the members of the SS before 1933, characterised them 'as "bruisers" and misfits, the unemployed and unemployable' and 'fragments of the old German elite' [78: *281*]. Writing a few years later, Heinz Höhne, on the basis of guesswork rather than any firm empirical evidence, came to the conclusion that the 'founders of the SS had come from lower-middle-class suburbia', while after 1929 it was ap-parently the 'the lost souls of the middle and upper-middle classes' who joined the SS [63: *54*]. In his major work on the SS published in the early 1980s, Koehl asserted – again on the basis of virtually

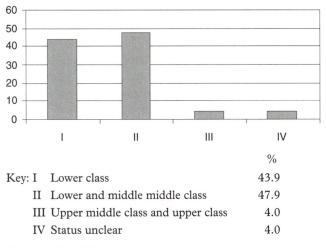

%

Key: I   Lower class   43.9
II Lower and middle middle class   47.9
III Upper middle class and upper class   4.0
IV Status unclear   4.0

Source: [102: *189*].

Figure 12   The social ranking of the membership of the SS enrolled between 1929 and 30 January 1933 according to Mühlberger (N: 496)

no firm evidence – that it was 'the lower middle class from which the SS drew its membership' [79: *82*]. Kater cited Höhne to support his view that 'in the first four years after the formation of the NSDAP, the SS did not differentiate itself in its sociology from the SA (or from the NSDAP), that is, it was similarly lower-middle-class in character' [71: *344*]. He did, however, advance some fragmentary evidence which suggested that the SS began to secure more support from the upper middle class and upper class in the early 1930s.

Except for some very limited data available on the membership of the SS in Munich and in Ludwigshafen in the early 1930s [101: *117–18*], the data summarised in Figure 12 on various SS units recruiting between 1929 and the end of January 1933 in the states of Bavaria, Bremen, Hesse and Oldenburg, and the provinces of Hanover, Hesse-Nassau and Rhineland in Prussia represents the first solid empirical evidence on the occupational and class background of rank-and-file members of the SS [102: *186–9*]. Given that the SS recruited members from the SA in some numbers in the late 1920s and early 1930s, the sizeable working-class presence within its ranks can perhaps be expected. Further evidence on various SS units recruited in the Rhineland region, in which over 50 per cent of the membership was provided by unskilled, semi-skilled and skilled manual workers before 30 January 1933, suggests that a strong presence of workers in this so-called 'elite' organisation in the 1920s and 1930s is probably correct [7: *218*]. It is likely that the discovery of data on other SS units will confirm that the social types attracted to the SS before 1933 were not restricted, as the older literature has it, to *Mittelstand* and upper-class elements.

The social profile of the membership of one other Nazi specialist organisation which acquired a mass base before the Nazi seizure of power, that of the NSBO, has also been subjected to evaluation of late. In existence since the mid-1920s, the factory cells organised by Nazi activists in various parts of Germany – primarily in Berlin and in the Ruhr region – targeted both blue-collar workers and white-collar employees. The NSBO was still a very small organisation with approximately 3,000 members by the time it became officially recognised as the party's trade union in January 1931. Even by the end of 1931 it mustered no more than 43,000 members. It was only to become an organisation of some size in the course of 1932, when it increased its membership to 170,000 by the late summer. By January 1933 its membership had grown to exceed the 300,000 mark [77: *170*].

For decades held to have had success only in mobilising primarily white-collar employees, the nature of the NSBO and the class status of its membership has been subjected to significant revision from the 1970s [77; 80; 92]. On the basis of fragmentary evidence, Gunther Mai pointed to marked regional variations in the composition of the NSBO and to the 'gradual shift from white-collar employees to blue-collar workers' within its ranks [92: *598*]. In the sole detailed analysis of the membership of the NSBO available, which is based on the around 50,000 members active in the NSBO in Berlin by early 1933, Volker Kratzenberg reached the conclusion that the NSBO had a broad social base, with a substantial part (it is not specifically quantified) of its membership coming from blue-collar workers [80: *236–9*].

The evidence available on the social characteristics of the rank-and-file membership of the HJ, SA, SS and NSBO suggests that these organisations were instrumental in widening the social base on which the Nazi Movement rested. The membership of the SA and HJ certainly was significantly more working class in nature than that of the party itself. The totally male HJ, SA and SS, as well as the predominantly male NSBO, appear to have penetrated quite effectively into the working class. These specialist organisations recruited tens of thousands, and, in the case of the SA and NSBO, hundreds of thousands, of working-class members to the Nazi cause. Collectively they overshadowed the efforts of such specialist organisations as the National Socialist Teachers' League (*Nationalsozialistischer Lehrerbund* – NSLB), the League of National Socialist German Lawyers (*Bund Nationalsozialistischer Deutscher Juristen* – BNSDJ) and the National Socialist German Doctors' League (*Nationalsozialistischer Deutscher Ärztebund* – NSDÄB), which drew thousands of middle- and upper-class individuals into the Nazi Party. Little is known as yet about the social background of the membership of a number of other Nazi specialist organisations, such as the National Socialist Women's League (*Nationalsozialistische Frauenschaft* – NSF).

Whereas the social characteristics of the rank-and-file membership of such organisations as the SA, SS, HJ and NSBO have been the focus of much dispute over the years, there is general consensus among historians and social scientists that the leadership of these organisations, indeed the leadership of virtually all of the many specialist organisations formed by the Nazis by 1933, was predominantly in the hands of individuals drawn from the middle class, and to a considerable extent also from the upper class. The leadership corps of the SA was certainly markedly different in social terms from the predominantly working-class background of the SA troopers [22; 43: *58–60*; 68]. As far as the higher echelons of the SA are concerned (those who reached the rank of *Standartenführer* or SA colonel and above), the meticulously researched, sophisticated quantitative analysis produced by Mathilde Jamin demonstrates that before the Nazi seizure of power, the higher ranks of the SA leadership corps were the almost exclusive preserve of the middle class and elite (see Figure 13), with few workers reaching the higher ranks of an organisation which had a predominantly working-class rank-and-file. It was only in the lower SA leadership positions, up to the rank of *Scharführer* (SA sergeant), which were generally staffed by individuals recruited from the rank-and-file membership, that the social gulf existing between the ordinary SA trooper and

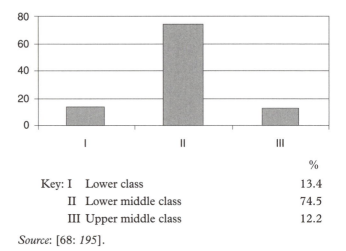

Key: I   Lower class   13.4
     II Lower middle class   74.5
     III Upper middle class   12.2

Source: [68: *195*].

Figure 13   The social ranking of the leadership of the SA before 1933 according to Jamin (N: 951)

the higher leadership corps of the SA was hardly in evidence [43: *59*]. Fischer notes that it was the complexity of the administrative tasks which were performed by the middle- and higher-ranking SA leaders which generally excluded the less educated from advancing within the SA hierarchy beyond the non-commissioned officer level [43: *61*].

The available evidence on the social configuration of the SS leadership throws up significant differences of views on the extent of the working-class presence within the SS officer corps. Kater points to the sizeable number of academics, especially doctors and lawyers, as well as 'aristocrats', among the SS leadership in the 1930s, the great bulk of whom rushed to join the SS after Hitler became chancellor [71: *372–3*]. The detailed study of the SS officer corps by Gunnar Boehnert, based on a sample of 5,250 SS leaders recruited in the period 1925 to 1939, highlights not only the overwhelmingly middle-class nature of the SS leadership corps by 1939, but the quite dramatic surge of academics into the SS hierarchy after the Nazi seizure of power. Boehnert's data suggests that only 7.4 per cent of the SS leaders in post in 1939 had a working-class background, whereas 52.6 per cent were from the lower middle class, and 40 per cent from the upper middle class [14: *362*]. A somewhat

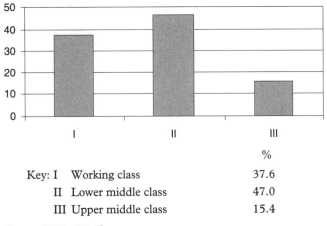

	%
Key: I Working class	37.6
II Lower middle class	47.0
III Upper middle class	15.4

Source: [137: *130–2*].

Figure 14 The class standing of leaders of the General-SS who had joined the SS before 30 January 1933 according to Ziegler (N: not given)

different picture of the social background of the SS leadership is provided by Herbert Ziegler. SS leaders drawn from the working class are much more numerous in his sample of 1,895 SS officers who were in post in 1938. Although he underlines that 75 per cent of the SS leadership involved individuals drawn from the lower and upper middle class, Ziegler also draws attention to the 25 per cent of leaders who had a working-class background, giving the SS leadership a 'heterogeneous structure' on the eve of the Second World War [137: *104–5, 118*]. Among the leaders of the General-SS recruited before 1933, moreover, those whom Ziegler defines as 'having working-class roots' (to measure the social standing of the SS leaders, Ziegler used the following variables for each leader: the social class of his father, the years of formal education he had received and the occupation which he had attained) were even more strongly represented, accounting for just under 38 per cent (see Figure 14) [137: *130*]. In the SS–TV (SS–*Totenkopfverbände* – SS–Death's Head Formations) the figure for leaders drawn from the working class was apparently higher still (43.4 per cent), whereas that for leaders with a working-class background in the SS–VT (SS–*Verfügungstruppe* – SS–Specialist Troops) was somewhat lower (31.2 per cent)

[137: *130*]. There is, however, general consensus on one feature of the SS leadership corps, namely that the higher the SS rank, the more likely that it was filled by better-educated individuals drawn from prestigious occupational backgrounds. Further research suggests itself to resolve the marked difference in the level of the working-class presence within the SS leadership which Boehnert and Ziegler obtained from their respective samples.

The leadership cadre of other Nazi specialist organisations has not been subjected to the careful scrutiny given those in charge of the SA and SS, but the indications are that these also drew the bulk of their leaders from the middle class and elite. Given the social make-up of the rank-and-file HJ, Stachura found the contrast between its strongly proletarian membership and bourgeois leadership particularly striking. On the basis of an analysis of 200 of the most significant HJ leaders active in the pre-1934 period, Stachura found that only 13 individuals (or 10.8 per cent) of the 120 he was able to classify in social terms came from the working class, while the rest all had middle-class backgrounds [124: *59*]. Similarly, despite the overall dominance of the working class in the HJ in the Palatinate, the branch leadership was primarily in the hands of middle-class individuals, while the handful of upper-middle-class and upper-class elements recruited by the HJ in the region provided the *Gau* leadership [101: *110, 113*]. The same pattern is discernible in the NSBO, the leadership of which, according to Kratzenberg, was also primarily in the hands of 'the petit-bourgeois white-collar employee element' [80: *179*]. It does seem that despite the often significant working-class presence within the rank-and-file membership of the more sizeable and important Nazi specialist organisations, these generally drew their leadership corps from the *Mittelstand* and from the elite.

Chapter 7

The social geometry of the Nazi electorate, 1928–1933

The first attempts to reach some conclusions about the social geometry of the support mobilised by the Nazi Party date back to the
early 1930s and were invariably based on visual observations of the
voting behaviour of the German electorate. Close on the heels of
the Nazi breakthrough in the *Reichstag* election of September 1930,
Theodor Geiger reached the conclusion that the electoral success of
the Nazi Party was fundamentally due to the support it had received
from members of the 'old' and the 'new' middle classes [50], a view
he was later to repeat in his seminal work on the social structure of
the German population, which contained a chapter on the relationship between Nazism and the *Mittelstand* [51: *109–22*]. In a series
of articles Werner Stephan examined in an impressionistic manner
the trends discernible in the *Landtag* and *Reichstag* elections from
1930 onwards, in which he – like Geiger – pointed to the resilience
displayed by the Catholic Centre Party and its Bavarian off-shoot,
the Bavarian People's Party, the continued strength of the left-wing
vote and the dramatic collapse of support for the major bourgeois
parties. Stephan assumed that the demise of the bourgeois parties accounted for the growing electoral strength of the Nazi Party
[128–31]. The 'middle-class thesis' of Nazism was born on the back
of such visual comparisons, which were limited to revealing rather
obvious trends.

An exception to such studies lacking methodological rigour was
the sophisticated work – by the standards of the time – produced by
Rudolf Heberle. It was completed by him in 1934, but not published
until almost a decade later, and focused on Schleswig-Holstein, the
only electoral district in which the Nazi Party secured an absolute majority in a *Reichstag* election before 1933 [58–9]. Heberle

correlated the social structure of counties (*Kreise*) and local communities (*Gemeinden*) with the electoral results of these basic administrative units, and reached the conclusion that it was the Protestant rural and small-town middle class which turned to the Nazi Party in droves [58–9]. Similar views were expressed by Charles Loomis and J. Allen Beegle just after Heberle's results had been made public [87].

In the post-war period the thesis that the Nazi Party was the political rallying point of the radicalised rural and urban *Mittelstand* continued to be the norm, and was strengthened further in a series of influential writings not based on any stringent empirical analysis [16; 64–5; 85]. Lipset's characterisation of the ideal-typical Nazi voter in 1932 as 'a middle-class self-employed Protestant who lived either on a farm or in a small community' emphatically restated the 'middle-class thesis' of Nazism in 1960 [85: *149*]. Occasional attempts to query the consensus, such as the argument advanced by Reinhard Bendix that it was young voters and former nonvoters who primarily fed the Nazi vote – at least until the elections of 1932 – rather than former right-wing (*Mittelstand*) voters [8], came to nothing. Bendix, influenced by Lipset's arguments, eventually distanced himself from his 'revisionist' ideas. The revival of Bendix's old approach by O'Lessker [109] also had little impact, though it did generate the odd riposte [121]. But such occasional attacks failed to disturb the dominant 'middle-class thesis' until a number of methodologically more sophisticated major studies on the Nazi Party's electorate appeared in the early 1980s [26; 56; 57].

Although none of the first modern electoral analyses dealt with the whole of the Nazi electorate, which limited their representative nature, they did collectively challenge, and then gradually undermine, firmly entrenched views on the social composition of the Nazi electorate. From the mid-1970s onwards Thomas Childers began to publish a number of articles in which he painted a more differentiated picture of the voting behaviour of the middle classes [24–5]. In 1983 his major work on the Nazi electorate appeared, in which he emphasised that significant differences existed in the social composition of the Nazi electorate before and after 1930, and pointed to the party's ability to secure support from all social groupings. Childers noted that the 'new' middle class (white-collar workers) had a more limited presence in the party's electorate than the 'old' middle class (farmers, shopkeepers, self-employed artisans). As to the working class and its assumed or alleged virtual absence within the Nazi electorate, Childers reached the conclusion that although there was a negative correlation between Nazism and industrial workers, there existed a positive one between Nazism and blue-collar workers in crafts and small enterprises, though this weakened somewhat after 1930 [24; 26]. In the summary of his findings, Childers emphasised that 'support for National Socialism varied in duration and degree', but that it was not 'confined to the lower middle class or to socially marginal *déclassé*'. He underlined, however, that 'the nucleus of the NSDAP's following was formed by the small farmers, shopkeepers, and independent artisans of the old middle class, who constituted the most stable and consistent components of the National Socialist constituency between 1924 and 1932' [26: *264*].

Childers suggested that the Nazi Party did evolve into a form of *Volkspartei*, a 'catch-all party' which gathered together the discontented from all social classes over time. But his book does not contain the sort of outspoken critique of the lower-middle-class thesis which is to be found in two further major studies on the Nazi electorate by Richard Hamilton and by Dirk Hänisch, which also appeared in the early 1980s. Hamilton's route to finding out who voted for the Nazi Party – given that he made clear that he was not enamoured with a purely statistical approach – was quite different to that taken by Childers and Hänisch. Rather than dealing with the electorate in part or as a whole, Hamilton's focus was restricted to towns with a population of 100,000 and over. He dealt with fifteen of fifty-two such sized towns in Germany in the 1920s, and pursued a question previously neglected in electoral analyses, the voting pattern of the upper middle class and upper class, that is, of the 'elite' of German society. Hamilton found that 'the best districts' – that is districts in which the upper middle class and upper class formed the majority of the population – of all but three of the cities which he investigated (the exceptions were Cologne, Munich and Frankfurt) 'gave Hitler and his party the strongest support' [56: *421*]. Another result of Hamilton's enquiry was that he found that in some towns a quarter of the electorate in working-class districts gave their vote to the Nazi Party [56: *386*]. Hamilton argued that the German equivalent of the 'Tory working-class voter' provided a considerable part of the NSDAP's electoral strength. Hamilton's conclusions, however, are undermined by the smallness of the urban 'sample' on which they are based, which inevitably limits the representative nature of his findings [94: *175*]. The significance of his work is further reduced by his failure, barring the exception provided by Berlin, to look at large towns situated in middle and eastern Germany. Nor did Hamilton examine the elite in any city in its entirety, for he only concentrated on the socially most homogeneous districts of the cities he had selected, ignoring the upper-class elements resident in other – more socially mixed – areas [94: *176*]. It was the strong presence of the elite – as well as the significant working-class presence – in the Nazi electorate in the relatively few towns which Hamilton examined which led him to reject the 'lower-middle-class' hypothesis of Nazism.

In a work based on a complex and sophisticated methodology reflecting state-of-the-art statistical techniques, Dirk Hänisch forcefully refuted the 'middle-class thesis'. He examined the behaviour of around 70 per cent of the German electorate stretching over the seven *Reichstag* elections spanning the years 1924 to 1933. Hänisch reached the conclusion that 'the confessional influence on electoral behaviour is one of the most important factors' [57: *224*] determining the extent of the Nazi vote, with religion acting as a block to Nazi penetration into the Catholic electorate in the rural areas in particular. Hänisch found that in the urban centres it was the left which acted as a brake on Nazi expansion. In the summary of his research Hänisch adamantly rejected the 'middle-class thesis', and concluded that 'the social basis of the NSDAP was fuelled by all strata' and that the party had 'a trans-class character'. Although he acknowledged the strong presence of the middle-class voter within the Nazi electorate, he rejected the thesis 'that the electorate of the NSDAP was formed *predominantly* by the middle class' [57: *228*].

Courtney Brown broke new ground in 1982 when he analysed the vote of all of the 946 counties of the Weimar Republic, though only for the *Reichstag* election of July 1932. Brown concluded that the Nazi electorate was confined to only sections of the Protestant lower middle class in that 'the highly flaunted Protestant petty bourgeois support seems to have occurred mainly in the rural areas', whereas Protestant urban areas were not bastions of petty bourgeois Nazi support. On the basis of his analysis, Brown reached the startling conclusion that 'the Nazis gained strong support from

the petty bourgeoisie in Catholic (urban) areas', and that as far as
the limited working-class support for Nazism was concerned, this
was confined to Catholic workers in the areas of trade and trans-
portation, who gave 'some support' to the Nazis, whereas Protestant
workers opposed them [19: *300–2*].

None of the important works summarised above offered a totally representative analysis of the whole of the Nazi electorate in
the Weimar Republic. That had to await the publication in 1991
of the authoritative study on the Nazi electorate by Jürgen Falter,
the product of two decades or more of primary research by Falter
and his research team. Falter and his colleagues began to produce a stream of informative publications on various aspects of the
Nazi electorate from the early 1980s [30–2; 34–7; 40]. Like Childers
and Hänisch (who was part of the 'Falter team' from 1984 to
1989), Falter pointed to the fact that there was no such thing as
a 'typical' Nazi voter, that the social configuration of the Nazi electorate was complex and that the 'middle-class thesis' was not tenable
in the light of the evidence. Important among the extensive output
by Falter and his fellow researchers is an article by Falter and
Hänisch which appeared in 1986, which demonstrated the strong
working-class support enjoyed by the Nazi Party at the polls from
the *Reichstag* election of 1928 onwards [37].

In his exhaustive study of the Nazi voter which appeared in 1991,
Falter examined all of the *Reichstag* elections, as well as the presidential elections of 1925 and 1932, and looked at the voters who
supported the Nazi Party from virtually every conceivable angle.
The results obtained through state-of-the-art statistical techniques
are contained in a bewildering array of tables and figures to be
found throughout the book. It is unlikely that a more comprehensive and statistically more complex analysis of the Nazi voter will
see the light of day in the foreseeable future. Falter reached the firm
conclusion that in electoral terms the Nazi Party was very much
a '*Volkspartei* of Protest' in every election from 1928 to 1933 (see
Figure 15). The most startling aspect of Falter's work is his finding
that a quite sizeable number of workers voted for Nazism. According
to his analysis working-class voters provided between 39 and 40 per
cent of the Nazi Party's vote in every *Reichstag* election from May
1928 to November 1932. Falter's calculations suggest that among
these Nazi working-class voters there were some 2 million former

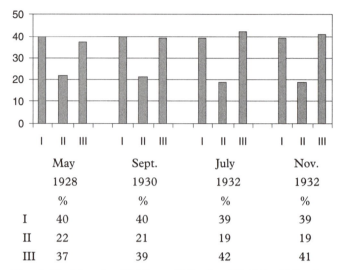

	May 1928 %	Sept. 1930 %	July 1932 %	Nov. 1932 %
I	40	40	39	39
II	22	21	19	19
III	37	39	42	41

Key: I: Working class II: New middle class III: Old middle class
Source: [32: *79*].

Figure 15   The social composition of the Nazi electorate in the *Reichstag* elections from 1928 to 1932 according to Falter

voters for the SPD by 1932, as well as approximately 350,000 former voters for the KPD [33: *116*]. Like Hänisch before him, Falter also points to the fact that it was the confessional factor, rather than class, that acted as the major block to the penetration of Nazism into the German body politic. In Catholic regions of Germany the Nazis found it difficult to generate the level of support that they were able to mobilise in Protestant regions [33: *175–9*]. This confessional immunisation was not universal, however. Falter himself notes that some 600,000 former voters for the Catholic Centre Party – and its Bavarian offshoot, the Bavarian People's Party – switched their allegiance to the Nazi Party between 1928 and 1933 [33: *116*]. It is also clear that there were quite a few villages and small towns in solidly Catholic regions of Germany in which the Nazis secured often very high returns in the elections of the early 1930s [61].

Collectively the modern studies on the Nazi voter highlight the marked social mix to be found in the Nazi electorate. Although voters drawn from the 'old' and 'new' middle class provided very strong support for the Nazis at the polls, with members of the 'old' middle class much more in evidence than those drawn from the 'new', the Nazi Party also gathered extensive support from the elite and from the working class. It is now generally accepted that the electoral support gathered by the Nazi Party came from very diverse social elements rather than just from the *Mittelstand*.

Chapter 8

Conclusion

A veritable revolution took place between the 1970s and the 1990s as far as our understanding of the social bases of Nazism is concerned. The end result of it has been the gradual undermining of the validity of the '(lower-) middle-class thesis' of Nazism which held sway for so long. Whereas Mühlberger's call for the abandonment of the 'middle-class thesis' [99: *504*] was dubbed 'folly' by Kater in the early 1980s [75: *236*], ten years later the latter had changed his view. By 1993 it was possible for Falter, a chief advocate of the 'people's party thesis' of Nazism, and Kater, a consistent advocate of the old orthodoxy which held that Nazism was a 'pre-eminently lower-middle-class affair', to write that 'a fundamental consensus has been established today as regards the main characteristics of the mass base on which the NSDAP rested . . . one that applies to the members as well as to the voters of Hitler's Party', namely that it had the characteristics of a 'people's party' [38: *155*]. The main contours of the social forces on which Nazism was based before 1933 are now fairly clearly established.

It is likely that future research will support and refine, rather than overturn, the consensus view which has emerged as far as the question of the social characteristics of Nazism is concerned. The cumulative result of all of the information now at hand has been the erosion of the acceptability of the *Mittelstandspartei* hypothesis to the point at which the validity of the alternative *Volkspartei* thesis can no longer be seriously questioned. From being the minority view, much decried in the pre- and post-war period, when the orthodox '(lower-) middle-class-thesis' of Nazism marginalised the 'people's party' or 'mass party' approach, the work of a number of scholars, especially Thomas Childers, Conan Fischer, Jürgen Falter,

Michael Kater (though perhaps not intentionally!), Paul Madden and Detlef Mühlberger, has produced empirically based statistical data which points overwhelmingly in one direction: that the Nazi Movement effectively transcended the class divide. Just as the dominance of the 'lower-middle-class theory' of the Nazi Party's membership was gradually demolished after 1980 by a series of studies based on empirical evidence, so the analyses of the electoral support enjoyed by the Nazis which have appeared since the early 1980s have shown that the predominating 'middle-class thesis' of the Nazi electorate cannot survive when tested by empirical means.

It is clear that the Nazis drew their members and voters from all segments of German society, though in unequal proportions. It was the ability of the Nazis to generate support from all social classes which ultimately gave the Nazi Movement its potency. There is general consensus among historians that the success of the Nazi Party did not just depend on its being 'a catch-all movement of protest' fuelled by the social and economic misery brought about by the World Depression. Although the collapse of the German economy was one factor behind the rapid surge in support which the Nazi Movement experienced from the late 1920s onwards – for the economic crisis undoubtedly generated growing and widespread resentment against a democratic state which seemed incapable of ameliorating the increasing distress of the mass of German society – the 'protest' aspect was but one dimension of a complex of factors which fed Nazism. Critical among these, and given greater potency by the successive economic and political crises from which the Weimar Republic suffered from its inception, was the Nazi Party's constantly proclaimed intention to create a classless *Volksgemeinschaft* (people's community) which would overcome the social and political divisions existing in German society. That idea, which had taken root in the German socialist movement in the years before the First World War, was appropriated by the Nazis in the 1920s, and undoubtedly exerted a strong appeal across the class divide, especially among working-class circles. The party's promise to tackle the social and economic problems facing *all* sections of society also generated broad support, as did the Nazi vision of a 'reborn', powerful Germany capable of playing a dominant role on the Continent once more. In the unrelenting propaganda of the Nazi Movement from the late 1920s onwards the party clearly articulated ideas which

many Germans of all occupational and social backgrounds found at-
tractive. The extreme racism on which the so-called *Weltanschauung*
of Nazism was based undoubtedly also moved sections of German
society to give their backing to the Nazi cause.

That elements of the *Mittelstand* responded strongly to the over-
tures of the Nazi Party to become the core of its constituency cannot
be denied and is clearly demonstrated by the available evidence.
But it is clear now that the *Mittelstand* was only marginally over-
represented in the Nazi Movement as a whole, given that it was
able to attract a surprisingly high level of support from the working
class, even if this class was under-represented within it in comparison to its size in society. It was the support from established social
circles, from the elite, which was significantly over-represented in
both the membership and – especially – the leadership of the Nazi
Movement. There is no denying that the *Mittelstand* and the elite
were more susceptible to Nazism's appeal than the working class,
but a party with a working-class content of around 40 per cent, supported at the polls by roughly the same percentage of working-class
voters, a party in which elite elements were increasingly conspicuous
after 1930, a movement which established specialist organisations –
such as the HJ, the SA, the SS and the NSBO – in which the working class provided the majority of the rank-and-file membership,
cannot be accommodated within the framework of the old 'middle-
class thesis'. This was recognised by a tiny minority during the
Weimar era, and even by Communists at the time, such as Hans
Jäger. He pointed out as early as 1932 that although middle-class
elements were over-represented in the membership of the NSDAP,
the party had nevertheless managed to mobilise a not insignificant
level of working-class support, especially from among its younger
age groups. He also observed that workers were especially prominent in the SA, and to a lesser extent the SS [66: *1430–1*]. Modern
research on the membership of the Nazi Party, its electorate and
the social composition of its most significant specialist organisations
has broadly arrived at the same conclusions which Jäger reached so
long ago. The NSDAP was indeed what the Nazis claimed it to be,
a *Volkspartei*, not a class or middle-class affair.

Bibliography

Listed is the critical *published* literature available in English, as well as a number of books and articles in German which are of special significance. Brief comments have been added to some references to explain the contribution made to the debate by the authors.

[1] Abel, T. (1938) *The Nazi Movement: Why Hitler Came to Power* (New York). An early attempt, using limited empirical data, to throw light on the social origins of the membership of the Nazi Party. Emphasises the middle-class nature of Nazism.

[2] Allen, W. S. (1966) *The Nazi Seizure of Power: The Experience of a Single German Town 1930–1935* (London).

[3] Allen, W. S. (1984) 'Farewell to Class Analysis in the Rise of Nazism: Comment', *Central European History*, 17, pp. 54–62.

[4] Andrews, H. D. (1986) 'The Social Composition of the NSDAP: Problems and Possible Solutions', *German Studies Review*, 9, pp. 293–318. Useful on coding procedures and problems surrounding the standardisation of social class models.

[5] Anheier, H. K. and Neidhardt, F. (1993) 'Soziographische Entwicklung der NSDAP in München 1925 bis 1930', in Bauer, R., Hockerts, H. G. and Ziegler, W. (eds.), *München – 'Hauptstadt der Bewegung'* (Munich), pp. 179–86.

[6] Banaszkiewicz, J. (1967) 'German Fascism and People of the Social Fringe', *Polish Western Affairs*, 8, pp. 251–88.

[7] Becker, A. and Mühlberger, D. (1999) 'Analysing the Sociography of the Membership of the *Schutzstaffel* (SS) in *SS-Oberabschnitt Rhein* using ACCESS II', *History and Computing*, 11, pp. 213–24.

[8] Bendix, R. (1952) 'Social Stratification and Political Power', *American Political Science Review*, 6, pp. 357–75.

[9] Bessel, R. (1984) *Political Violence and the Rise of Nazism: The Storm Troopers in Eastern Germany 1925–34* (New Haven and London).

[10] Bessel, R. and Jamin, M. (1979) 'Nazis, Workers and the Use of Quantitative Evidence', *Social History*, 4, pp. 111–16.

[11] Bessel, R. and Jamin, M. (1980) 'Statistics and the Historian: A Rejoinder', *Social History*, 1, pp. 139–40.

[12] Boak, H. (1989) '"Our Last Hope": Women's Votes for Hitler – a Re-appraisal', *German Studies Review*, 12, pp. 289–310.

[13] Boehnert, G. C. (1979) 'An Analysis of the Age and Education of the SS *Führerkorps*, 1925–1939', *Historical Social Research*, 12, pp. 4–17.

[14] Boehnert, G. C. (1981) 'The Jurists in the SS-*Führerkorps*, 1925–1939', in Hirschfeld, G. and Kettenacker, L. (eds.), *Der 'Führerstaat': Mythos und Realität. Studien zur Struktur und Politik des Dritten Reiches* (Stuttgart), pp. 361–74.

[15] Böhnke, W. (1974) *Die NSDAP im Ruhrgebiet 1920–1933* (Bonn and Bad Godesberg).

[16] Bracher, K. D. (1973) *The German Dictatorship: The Origins, Structure and Consequences of National Socialism* (London).

[17] Broszat, M. (1981) *The Hitler State: The Foundation and Development of the Internal Structure of the Third Reich* (London and New York).

[18] Browder, G. C. (1975) 'Potentials of the Berlin Document Center', *Central European History*, 5, pp. 275–92.

[19] Brown, C. (1982) 'The Nazi Vote: A National Ecological Study', *American Political Science Review*, 76, pp. 285–302. An analysis of the Nazi vote limited to the *Reichstag* election of July 1932. The statistical method employed in the analysis is not made clear.

[20] Brustein, W. (1996) *The Logic of Evil: The Social Origins of the Nazi Party, 1925–1933* (New Haven and London). Employs 'rational choice' theory to explain why the majority of the members joined the Nazi Party. Argues that the NSDAP was a *Volkspartei* in social terms.

[21] Brustein, W. and Falter, J. W. (1995) 'Who Joined the Nazi Party? Assessing Theories of the Social Origins of Nazism', *Zeitgeschichte*, 3–4, pp. 83–108.

[22] Campbell, B. (1998) *The SA Generals and the Rise of Nazism* (Lexington).

[23] Carsten, F. L. (1967) *The Rise of Fascism* (London).

[24] Childers, T. (1976) 'The Social Bases of the National Socialist Vote', *Journal of Contemporary History*, 11, pp. 17–42.

[25] Childers, T. (1980) 'National Socialism and the New Middle Class', in Mann, R. (ed.), *Die Nationalsozialisten: Analysen faschistischer Bewegungen* (Stuttgart), pp. 19–33.

[26] Childers, T. (1983) *The Nazi Voter: The Social Foundations of Fascism in Germany, 1919–1933* (Chapel Hill and London). One of the first major attempts to get to grips with the social contours of the Nazi

voter. Based on an unrepresentative sample involving around 50 per cent of the electorate. Examines all of the *Reichstag* elections from 1924 to 1932, and concludes that the Nazis secured support from all social classes. Provides a most useful insight into the Nazi propaganda campaigns preceding each election.

[27] Childers, T. (1984) 'Who, Indeed, Voted for Hitler?', *Central European History*, 17, pp. 45–53.

[28] Doblin, E. M. and Pohly, C. (1945/6) 'The Social Composition of the Nazi Leadership', *American Journal of Sociology*, 51, pp. 42–9.

[29] Douglas, D. M. (1977) 'The Parent Cell: Some Computer Notes on the Composition of the First Nazi Party Group in Munich 1919–1921', *Central European History*, 10, pp. 55–62.

[30] Falter, J. W. (1981) 'Radicalization of the Middle Classes or Mobilization of the Unpolitical? The Theories of Seymour Martin Lipset and Reinhard Bendix on the Electoral Support of the NSDAP in the Light of Recent Research', *Social Science Information*, 20, pp. 389–430.

[31] Falter, J. W. (1986) 'The National Socialist Mobilisation of New Voters: 1928–1933', in Childers, T. (ed.), *The Formation of the Nazi Constituency 1919–1933* (London and Sydney), pp. 202–31.

[32] Falter, J. W. (1990) 'The First German Volkspartei: The Social Foundations of the NSDAP', in Rohe, K. (ed.), *Elections, Parties and Political Traditions: Social Foundations of German Parties and Party Systems, 1867–1987* (New York, Oxford and Munich), pp. 53–81.

[33] Falter, J. W. (1991) *Hitlers Wähler* (Munich). The product of some two decades or so of intensive research on the Nazi voter. Argues that the Nazi Party was a 'people's party of protest' drawing support from all social classes. The definitive study on the sociology of the Nazi electorate. Probably the last word on the subject for the foreseeable future.

[34] Falter, J. W. (1992) 'Economic Debts and Political Gains: Electoral Support for the Nazi Party in Agrarian and Commercial Sectors, 1928–1933', *Historical Social Research*, 17, pp. 3–21.

[35] Falter, J. W. (1996) 'How Likely Were Workers to Vote for the NSDAP?', in Fischer, C. (ed.), *The Rise of National Socialism and the Working Classes in Weimar Germany* (Providence and Oxford), pp. 9–45.

[36] Falter, J. W. (1996) 'The Young Membership of the NSDAP between 1925 and 1933: A Demographic and Social Profile', in Fischer, C. (ed.), *The Rise of National Socialism and the Working Classes in Weimar Germany* (Providence and Oxford), pp. 79–98.

[37] Falter, J. W. and Hänisch, D. (1986) 'Die Anfälligkeit von Arbeitern gegenüber der NSDAP bei den Reichstagswahlen 1928–1933', *Archiv für Sozialgeschichte*, 26, pp. 179–216.

[38] Falter, J. W. and Kater, M. H. (1993) 'Wähler und Mitglieder der NSDAP: Neue Forschungsergebnisse zur Soziographie des Nationalsozialismus 1925 bis 1933', *Geschichte und Gesellschaft*, 19, pp. 155–77.

[39] Falter, J. W. and Mühlberger, D. (1999) 'The Anatomy of a *Volkspartei*: The Sociography of the Membership of the NSDAP in *Stadt-* and *Landkreis* Wetzlar, 1925–1933', *Historical Social Research*, 24, pp. 58–98.

[40] Falter, J. W. and Zintl, R. (1988) 'The Economic Crisis of the 1930s and the Nazi Vote', *Journal of Interdisciplinary History*, 19, pp. 55–85.

[41] Fischer, C. (1978) 'The Occupational Background of the SA's Rank and File Membership during the Depression Years 1929 to mid-1934', in Stachura, P. (ed.), *The Shaping of the Nazi State* (London), pp. 131–59. An important article which points to the strong working-class presence within the SA.

[42] Fischer, C. (1982) 'The SA of the NSDAP: Social Background and Ideology of the Rank and File in the Early 1930s', *Journal of Contemporary History*, 17, pp. 651–70.

[43] Fischer, C. (1983) *Stormtroopers: A Social, Economic and Ideological Analysis, 1929–35* (London). A pioneering study on the social background of the membership of the SA. Argues that the rank-and-file of the organisation was predominantly working class in its composition, whereas the bulk of the SA leadership was drawn from the middle class.

[44] Fischer, C. and Hicks, C. (1980) 'Statistics and the Historian: The Occupational Profile of the SA of the NSDAP', *Social History*, 5, pp. 131–8.

[45] Fischer, C. and Mühlberger, D. (1996) 'The Pattern of the SA's Social Appeal', in Fischer, C. (ed.), *The Rise of National Socialism and the Working Classes in Weimar Germany* (Providence and Oxford), pp. 99–113. Based on a very broad array of empirical evidence, the authors argue that the SA was a predominantly working-class organisation.

[46] Franz-Willing, G. (1962) *Die Hitlerbewegung, der Ursprung 1919–1922* (Hamburg and Berlin).

[47] Friters, G. (1932) 'Who Are the German Fascists', *Current History*, 35, pp. 532–6.

[48] Fritz, S. G. (1987) 'The NSDAP a Volkspartei? A Look at the Social Basis of the Nazi Voter', *History Teacher*, 20, pp. 379–99.

[49] Geary, D. (1998) 'Who Voted for the Nazis?', *History Today*, 48, pp. 8–14.

[50] Geiger, T. (1930) 'Panik im Mittelstand', *Die Arbeit*, 7, pp. 637–54.

[51] Geiger, T. (1932) *Die Soziale Schichtung des deutschen Volkes: Ein soziographischer Versuch auf statistischer Grundlage* (Darmstadt).

Contains a chapter on the relationship between the *Mittelstand* and Nazism.

[52] Genuneit, J. (1980) 'Methodische Probleme der quantitativen Analyse früher NSDAP-Mitgliederlisten', in Mann, R. (ed.), *Die Nationalsozialisten: Analysen faschistischer Bewegungen* (Stuttgart), pp. 34–66.

[53] Gerth, H. (1940) 'The Nazi Party: Its Leadership and Composition', *American Journal of Sociology*, 45, pp. 517–41.

[54] Gordon, H. J., Jr (1972) *Hitler and the Beer Hall Putsch* (Princeton).

[55] Grill, J. H. (1983) *The Nazi Movement in Baden, 1920–1945* (Chapel Hill).

[56] Hamilton, R. F. (1982) *Who Voted for Hitler?* (Princeton). Emphasises the strong support which the Nazis secured from the elite in the more affluent districts of a number of German cities. Also points to the support given to Nazism by the working class. Questions the validity of the 'lower-middle-class thesis' of Nazism.

[57] Hänisch, D. (1983) *Sozialstrukturelle Bestimmungsgründe des Wahlverhaltens in der Weimarer Republik: Eine Aggregatdatenanalyse der Ergebnisse der Reichstagswahlen 1924–1933* (Duisburg). One of the first major studies on the electorate of the Nazi Party. A very sophisticated analysis which deals with all of the *Reichstag* elections between 1924 and 1933. Concludes that the Nazi Party acquired voters from all social classes and that the 'middle-class thesis' of Nazism is not tenable.

[58] Heberle, R. (1943) 'The Political Movements among the Rural People in Schleswig-Holstein, 1918 to 1932', *Journal of Politics*, 5, pp. 3–26.

[59] Heberle, R. (1945) *From Democracy to Dictatorship: A Regional Case Study on Political Parties in Germany* (Baton Rouge). A pioneering regional study investigating the social forces which fed Nazism in rural Schleswig-Holstein.

[60] Heiden, K. (1935) *A History of National Socialism* (New York).

[61] Heilbronner, O. and Mühlberger, D. (1997) 'The Achilles' Heel of German Catholicism: "Who Voted for Hitler?" Revisited', *European History Quarterly*, 27, pp. 221–49. The authors point to the often very high level of support which the Nazi Party secured in some Catholic villages and small towns in various regions of Germany.

[62] Heuss, T. (1932) *Hitlers Weg* (Stuttgart).

[63] Höhne, H. (1980) *The Order of the Death's Head: The Story of Hitler's SS* (London).

[64] Holzer, Jerzy (1970) 'La portée sociale du N.S.D.A.P. dans les années 1928–1930', *Acta Poloniae Historica*, 22, pp. 283–93.

[65] Holzer, Jerzy (1975) *Parteien und Massen: Die politische Krise in Deutschland 1928–1930* (Wiesbaden).

[66] Jäger, H. (1932) 'Der Faschismus in Deutschland', *Internationale Pressekorrespondenz*, No. 44, pp. 1355–8; No. 45, pp. 1389–92; No. 46, pp. 1427–31; No. 47, pp. 1477–87; No. 48, pp. 1533–4; No. 49, pp. 1555–6.

[67] Jamin, M. (1978) 'Zur Kritik an Michael Katers Überlegungen über Quantifizierung und NS-Geschichte', *Geschichte und Gesellschaft*, 4, pp. 536–41.

[68] Jamin, M. (1984) *Zwischen den Klassen: Zur Sozialstruktur der SA-Führerschaft* (Wuppertal). The definitive study on the social characteristics of the leadership of the SA.

[69] Jensen-Butler, B. (1976) 'An Outline of a Weberian Analysis of Class with Particular Reference to the Middle Class and the NSDAP in Weimar Germany', *British Journal of Sociology*, 27, pp. 50–60.

[70] Kater, M. H. (1971) 'Zur Soziographie der frühen NSDAP, *Vierteljahrshefte für Zeitgeschichte*, 19, pp. 124–60. An important early quantitative analysis of the social contours of the membership of the Nazi Party recruited on the eve of the Munich Putsch. Argues that the Nazi Party was a lower-middle-class phenomenon. This conclusion is arrived at through the use of an unrealistic class model, in which the working class is restricted to unskilled workers only.

[71] Kater, M. H. (1973) 'Zum gegenseitigen Verhältnis von SA und SS in der Sozialgeschichte des Nationalsozialismus von 1925 bis 1939', *Vierteljahrshefte für Sozial- und Wirtschaftsgeschichte*, 62, pp. 339–79.

[72] Kater, M. H. (1976) 'Ansätze zu einer Soziologie der SA bis zur Röhmkrise', in Engelhardt, U., Sellin, V. and Stuke, H. (eds.), *Soziale Bewegung und politische Verfassung. Beiträge zur Geschichte der modernen Welt* (Stuttgart), pp. 798–831.

[73] Kater, M. H. (1977) 'Quantifizierung und NS-Geschichte: Methodologische Überlegungen über Grenzen und Möglichkeiten einer EDV-Analyse der NSDAP-Sozialstruktur von 1925 bis 1945', *Geschichte und Gesellschaft*, 3, pp. 453–84.

[74] Kater, M. H. (1980) 'Methodologische Überlegungen über Möglichkeiten und Grenzen einer Analyse der sozialen Zusammensetzung der NSDAP von 1925 bis 1945', in Mann, R. (ed.), *Die Nationalsozialisten: Analysen faschistischer Bewegungen* (Stuttgart), pp. 155–85.

[75] Kater, M. H. (1983) *The Nazi Party: A Social Profile of Members and Leaders, 1919–1945* (Oxford). The first major analysis of the rank-and-file membership and leadership of the Nazi Party. A very important work covering the NSDAP from the time of its formation in 1919 to its collapse in 1945. Argues that the Nazi Party was a 'pre-eminently lower-middle-class phenomenon'.

[76] Kater, M. H. (1985) 'Generationskonflikt als Entwicklungsfaktor in der NS-Bewegung vor 1933', *Geschichte und Gesellschaft*, 11, pp. 217–43.

[77] Kele, M. (1972) *Nazis and Workers: National Socialist Appeals to German Labor, 1919–1933* (Chapel Hill). A useful in-depth analysis of the type of propaganda generated by the Nazi Party in its efforts to attract blue-collar workers in the 1920s and early 1930s.

[78] Koehl, R. L. (1962) 'The Character of the Nazi SS', *Journal of Modern History*, 34, pp. 275–83.

[79] Koehl, R. L. (1983) *The Black Corps: The Structure and Power Struggles of the Nazi SS* (Madison).

[80] Kratzenberg, V. (1987) *Arbeiter auf dem Weg zu Hitler? Die Nationalsozialistische Betriebszellen-Organisation. Ihre Entstehung, ihre Programmatik, ihr Scheitern 1927–1934* (Frankfurt am Main, Bern and New York). The first major work on the NSBO to deal with the social basis of this organisation in some depth. Shows that in the Berlin region the NSBO was able to secure strong support in the early 1930s from both blue-collar and white-collar workers.

[81] Kreuz, S. and Mühlberger, D. (2001) 'Die Soziographie der Mitgliedschaft der NSDAP in Offenbach a. M., 1925–1935', *Offenbacher Geschichtsblätter*, 44, pp. 126–45.

[82] Kuechler, M. (1992) 'The NSDAP Vote in the Weimar Republic: An Assessment of the State-of-the-Art in View of Modern Electoral Research', *Historical Social Research*, 17, pp. 22–52. Critically reviews the modern literature on the social characteristics of the Nazi electorate and argues that it modifies, rather than refutes, the 'lower-middle-class thesis'. Sceptical about results dependent solely on statistical analysis.

[83] Lasswell, H. D. (1933) 'The Psychology of Hitlerism', *Political Quarterly*, 14, pp. 373–84.

[84] Lerner, D. (1951) *The Nazi Elite* (Stanford).

[85] Lipset, S. M. (1960) *Political Man* (New York).

[86] Loewenberg, P. (1971) 'The Psychohistorical Origins of the Nazi Youth Cohort', *American Historical Review*, 75, pp. 1457–502.

[87] Loomis, C. P. and Beegle, J. A. (1946) 'The Spread of German Nazism in Rural Areas', *American Sociological Review*, 11, pp. 724–34.

[88] Madden, P. (1982) 'Some Social Characteristics of Early Nazi Party Members, 1919–23', *Central European History*, 15, pp. 34–56. An important article by a staunch advocate of the view that the Nazi Party drew its support from all social classes.

[89] Madden, P. (1982) 'Generational Aspects of German National Socialism, 1919–33', *Social Science Quarterly*, 63, pp. 445–61.

[90] Madden, P. (1982) 'Who Were the Nazis? A Survey of Historical Opinion', *Red River Valley Historical Journal of World History*, 6, pp. 33–53.

[91] Madden, P. (1987) 'The Social Class Origins of Nazi Party Members as Determined by Occupations, 1919–1933', *Social Science Quarterly*, 68, pp. 263–79. An important article based on the largest sample taken from the BDC to date. Argues that the Nazi Party was a *Volkspartei*.

[92] Mai, G. (1983) 'Die Nationalsozialistische Betriebszellen-Organisation: Zum Verhältnis von Arbeiterschaft und Nationalsozialismus', *Vierteljahrshefte für Zeitgeschichte*, 31, pp. 573–613.

[93] Mai, G. (1985) 'Zwischen den Klassen? Zur Soziographie der SA', *Archiv für Sozialgeschichte*, 25, pp. 634–46.

[94] Manstein, P. (1990) *Die Mitglieder und Wähler der NSDAP 1919–1933: Untersuchungen zu ihrer schichtmäßigen Zusammensetzung* (Frankfurt am Main, Bern, New York and Paris). Lists a whole catalogue of methodological shortcomings and mistakes made by historians and social scientists who have worked on the sociology of Nazism. Provides a comprehensive summary of the literature available on the sociology of the membership and electorate of the Nazi Party by the late 1980s.

[95] Maser, W. (1965) *Die Frühgeschichte der NSDAP: Hitlers Weg bis 1924* (Frankfurt am Main and Bonn).

[96] Merkl, P. H. (1975) *Political Violence under the Swastika: 581 Early Nazis* (Princeton). A detailed analysis of the Abel data collected in the early 1930s.

[97] Merkl, P. H. (1980) *The Making of a Stormtrooper* (Princeton).

[98] Merkl, P. H. (1980) 'Zur quantitativen Analyse von Lebensläufen Alter Kämpfer', in Mann, R. (ed.), *Die Nationalsozialisten: Analysen faschistischer Bewegungen* (Stuttgart), pp. 67–83.

[99] Mühlberger, D. (1980) 'The Sociology of the NSDAP: The Question of Working-Class Membership', *Journal of Contemporary History*, 15, pp. 493–511. Questions the validity of the 'middle-class thesis' of Nazism.

[100] Mühlberger, D. (1985) 'The Occupational and Social Structure of the NSDAP in the Border Province Posen-West Prussia in the Early 1930s', *European History Quarterly*, 15, pp. 281–311.

[101] Mühlberger, D. (1987) 'Germany', in *idem* (ed.), *The Social Basis of European Fascist Movements* (London, New York and Sydney), pp. 40–139.

[102] Mühlberger, D. (1991) *Hitler's Followers: Studies in the Sociology of the Nazi Movement* (London and New York). Examines the social contours of the Nazi Party in four different regions of Germany, as

well as the social characteristics of the membership of the SA and SS. A strong advocate of the *Volkspartei* thesis.

[103] Mühlberger, D. (1996) 'A "Workers' Party" or a "Party without Workers"? The Extent and Nature of the Working-Class Membership of the NSDAP, 1919–1933', in Fischer, C. (ed.), *The Rise of National Socialism and the Working Classes in Weimar Germany* (Providence and Oxford), pp. 47–77. Argues that a considerable number of workers – primarily of semi-skilled and skilled status – were attracted to Nazism before Hitler became chancellor at the end of January 1933.

[104] Mühlberger, D. (1999) 'A Social Profile of the Saxon NSDAP Membership before 1933', in Szejnmann, C.-C. W., *Nazism in Central Germany: The Brownshirts in 'Red' Saxony* (New York and Oxford), pp. 211–19. Points to the strong working-class presence within the ranks of the Nazi Party in *Gau* Saxony.

[105] Mühlberger, D. (2002) 'Who Were the Nazis? The Social Characteristics of the Support Mobilised by the Nazi Movement, 1920–1933', *History Teaching Review Year Book*, 16, pp. 22–31.

[106] Neumann, S. (1965) *Die Parteien der Weimarer Republik* (Stuttgart).

[107] Noakes, J. (1971) *The Nazi Party in Lower Saxony 1921–1933* (Oxford). A classic regional study.

[108] Noakes, J. (1995) 'Who Supported Hitler?', *Modern History Review*, 6, pp. 28–31.

[109] O'Lessker, K. (1968) 'Who Voted for Hitler? A New Look at the Class Basis of Nazism', *American Journal of Sociology*, 74, pp. 63–9.

[110] O'Loughlin, J., Flint, C. and Anselin, L. (1994) 'The Geography of the Nazi Vote: Context, Confession, and Class in the Reichstag Election of 1930', *Annals of the Association of American Geographers*, 84, pp. 351–80.

[111] Orlow, D. (1971) *The History of the Nazi Party, vol. I: 1919–33* (Newton Abbot).

[112] Paetel, K. O. (1954) 'Die SS: Ein Beitrag zur Soziologie des Nationalsozialismus', *Vierteljahrshefte für Zeitgeschichte*, 2, pp. 1–33.

[113] *Partei-Statistik: Stand 1. Januar 1935.* Herausgeber: Der Reichsorganisationsleiter der NSDAP (Munich).

[114] Pridham, G. (1973) *Hitler's Rise to Power: The Nazi Movement in Bavaria, 1923–1933* (London).

[115] Rebentisch, D. (1983) 'Persönlichkeitsprofil und Karriereverlauf der nationalsozialistischen Führungskader in Hessen, 1928–1945', *Hessisches Jahrbuch für Landesgeschichte*, 33, pp. 293–331.

[116] Reiche, E. G. (1986) *The Development of the SA in Nürnberg, 1922–1934* (Cambridge).

[117] Rogowski, R. (1977) 'The *Gauleiter* and the Social Origins of Fascism', *Comparative Studies in Society and History*, 19, pp. 399–430.

[118] Rothenberger, K.-H. (1986) 'Die NSDAP in der Pfalz: Sozialstruktur der Partei nach der Parteistatistik von 1935', *Jahrbuch Westdeutscher Landesgeschichte*, 12, pp. 199–211.

[119] Schäfer, W. (1957) *NSDAP: Entwicklung und Struktur der Staatspartei des Dritten Reiches* (Hanover and Frankfurt am Main).

[120] Schmidt, C. (1981) 'Zu den Motiven "alter Kämpfer" in der NSDAP', in Peukert, D. and Reulecke, J. (eds.), *Die Reihen fast geschlossen: Beiträge zur Geschichte des Alltags unterm Nationalsozialismus* (Wuppertal), pp. 21–43.

[121] Schnaiberg, A. (1968) 'A Critique of Karl O'Lessker's "Who Voted for Hitler?"', *American Journal of Sociology*, 74, pp. 732–5.

[122] Sering, P. (1936) 'Der Faschismus', *Zeitschrift für Sozialismus*, 24–5, pp. 765–92.

[123] 7771 Document Center OMGUS (1947) *Who was a Nazi? Facts about the Membership Procedure of the Nazi Party* (Berlin).

[124] Stachura, P. D. (1975) *Nazi Youth in the Weimar Republic* (Santa Barbara and Oxford).

[125] Stachura, P. D. (1983) 'The Nazis, the Bourgeoisie and the Workers during the *Kampfzeit*', in *idem* (ed.), *The Nazi Machtergreifung* (London), pp. 15–32.

[126] Stachura, P. D. (1983) 'The NSDAP and the German Working Class, 1925–1933', in Dobkowski, M. N. and Wallimann, I. (eds.), *Towards the Holocaust: The Social and Economic Collapse of the Weimar Republic* (Westport and London), pp. 131–53.

[127] Stachura, P. D. (1993) 'National Socialism and the German Proletariat, 1925–1935: Old Myths and New Perspectives', *Historical Journal*, 36, pp. 701–18.

[128] Stephan, W. (1931) 'Zur Soziologie der Nationalsozialistischen Deutschen Arbeiterpartei', *Zeitschrift für Politik*, 20, pp. 793–800.

[129] Stephan, W. (1932) 'Grenzen des nationalsozialistischen Vormarsches: Eine Analyse der Wahlziffern seit der Reichstagswahl 1930', *Zeitschrift für Politik*, 21, pp. 570–8.

[130] Stephan, W. (1933) 'Die Parteien nach den großen Frühjahrskämpfen: Eine Analyse der Wahlziffern des Jahres 1932', *Zeitschrift für Politik*, 22, pp. 110–18.

[131] Stephan, W. (1933) 'Die Reichstagswahlen vom 31. Juli 1932', *Zeitschrift für Politik*, 22, pp. 353–60.

[132] Stokes, L. D. (1978) 'The Social Composition of the Nazi Party in Eutin, 1925–1932', *International Review of Social History*, 23, pp. 1–32.

[133] Wernette, R. D. (1977) 'Quantitative Methods in Studying Political Mobilization in Late Weimar Germany', *Historical Methods Newsletter*, 10, pp. 97–101.

[134] Winkler, H. A. (1972) *Mittelstand, Demokratie und Nationalsozialis-mus: Die politische Entwicklung von Handwerk und Kleinhandel in der Weimarer Republik* (Cologne).

[135] Winkler, H. A. (1972) 'Extremismus der Mitte? Sozialgeschichtliche Aspekte der nationalsozialistischen Machtergreifung', *Viertel-jahrshefte für Zeitgeschichte*, 20, pp. 175–91.

[136] Winkler, H. A. (1976) 'Mittelstandsbewegung oder Volkspartei? Zur sozialen Basis der NSDAP', in Schieder, W. (ed.), *Faschismus als soziale Bewegung: Deutschland und Italien im Vergleich* (Hamburg), pp. 97–118.

[137] Ziegler, H. F. (1989) *Nazi Germany's New Aristocracy: The SS Lead-ership, 1925–1939* (Princeton). Argues that the SS leadership was characterised by heterogeneity, and that working-class elements pro-vided around one third of the SS leadership before 1933, and around one quarter of the SS leaders in 1939.

Index

New Studies in Economic and Social History

Titles in the series available from Cambridge University Press:

1. M. Anderson, *Approaches to the History of the Western Family,
   1500–1914*
   ISBN 0 521 55260 5 (hardback) 0 521 55793 3 (paperback)
2. W. Macpherson, *The Economic Development of Japan, 1868–1941*
   ISBN 0 521 55792 5 (hardback) 0 521 55261 3 (paperback)
3. R. Porter, *Disease, Medicine, and Society in England, 1550–1860*
   (second edition)
   ISBN 0 521 55262 1 (hardback) 0 521 55791 7 (paperback)
4. B. W. E. Alford, *British Economic Performance since 1945*
   ISBN 0 521 55263 X (hardback) 0 521 55790 9 (paperback)
5. A. Crowther, *Social Policy in Britain, 1914–1939*
   ISBN 0 521 55264 8 (hardback) 0 521 55789 5 (paperback)
6. E. Roberts, *Women's Work 1840–1940*
   ISBN 0 521 55265 6 (hardback) 0 521 55788 7 (paperback)
7. C. Ó Gráda, *The Great Irish Famine*
   ISBN 0 521 55266 4 (hardback) 0 521 55787 9 (paperback)
8. R. Rodger, *Housing in Urban Britain 1780–1914*
   ISBN 0 521 55267 2 (hardback) 0 521 55786 0 (paperback)
9. P. Slack, *The English Poor Law 1531–1782*
   ISBN 0 521 55268 0 (hardback) 0 521 55785 2 (paperback)
10. J. L. Anderson, *Explaining Long-term Economic Change*
    ISBN 0 521 55269 9 (hardback) 0 521 55784 4 (paperback)
11. D. Baines, *Emigration from Europe 1815–1930*
    ISBN 0 521 55270 2 (hardback) 0 521 55783 6 (paperback)
12. M. Collins, *Banks and Industrial Finance 1800–1939*
    ISBN 0 521 55271 0 (hardback) 0 521 55782 8 (paperback)

13. A. Dyer, *Decline and Growth in English Towns 1400–1640*
    ISBN 0 521 55272 9 (hardback) 0 521 55781 X (paperback)

14. R. B. Outhwaite, *Dearth, Public Policy and Social Disturbance in England, 1550–1800*
    ISBN 0 521 55273 7 (hardback) 0 521 55780 1 (paperback)

15. M. Sanderson, *Education, Economic Change and Society in England*
    ISBN 0 521 55274 5 (hardback) 0 521 55779 8 (paperback)

16. R. D. Anderson, *Universities and Elites in Britain since 1800*
    ISBN 0 521 55275 3 (hardback) 0 521 55778 X (paperback)

17. C. Heywood, *The Development of the French Economy, 1700–1914*
    ISBN 0 521 55276 1 (hardback) 0 521 55777 1 (paperback)

18. R. A. Houston, *The Population History of Britain and Ireland 1500–1750*
    ISBN 0 521 55277 X (hardback) 0 521 55776 3 (paperback)

19. A. J. Reid, *Social Classes and Social Relations in Britain 1850–1914*
    ISBN 0 521 55278 8 (hardback) 0 521 55775 5 (paperback)

20. R. Woods, *The Population of Britain in the Nineteenth Century*
    ISBN 0 521 55279 6 (hardback) 0 521 55774 7 (paperback)

21. T. C. Barker, *The Rise and Rise of Road Transport, 1700–1990*
    ISBN 0 521 55280 X (hardback) 0 521 55773 9 (paperback)

22. J. Harrison, *The Spanish Economy*
    ISBN 0 521 55281 8 (hardback) 0 521 55772 0 (paperback)

23. C. Schmitz, *The Growth of Big Business in the United States and Western Europe, 1850–1939*
    ISBN 0 521 55282 6 (hardback) 0 521 55771 2 (paperback)

24. R. A. Church, *The Rise and Decline of the British Motor Industry*
    ISBN 0 521 55283 4 (hardback) 0 521 55770 4 (paperback)

25. P. Horn, *Children's Work and Welfare, 1780–1880*
    ISBN 0 521 55284 2 (hardback) 0 521 55769 0 (paperback)

26. R. Perren, *Agriculture in Depression, 1870–1940*
    ISBN 0 521 55285 0 (hardback) 0 521 55768 2 (paperback)

27. R. J. Overy, *The Nazi Economic Recovery 1932–1938* (second edition)
    ISBN 0 521 55286 9 (hardback) 0 521 55767 4 (paperback)

28. S. Cherry, *Medical Services and the Hospitals in Britain, 1860–1939*
    ISBN 0 521 57126 X (hardback) 0 521 57784 5 (paperback)

29. D. Edgerton, *Science, Technology and the British Industrial 'Decline', 1870–1970*
    ISBN 0 521 57127 8 (hardback) 0 521 57778 0 (paperback)

30. C. A. Whatley, *The Industrial Revolution in Scotland*
    ISBN 0 521 57228 2 (hardback) 0 521 57643 1 (paperback)

31. H. E. Meller, *Towns, Plans and Society in Modern Britain*
    ISBN 0 521 57227 4 (hardback) 0 521 57644 X (paperback)
32. H. Hendrick, *Children, Childhood and English Society, 1880–1990*
    ISBN 0 521 57253 3 (hardback) 0 521 57624 5 (paperback)
33. N. Tranter, *Sport, Economy and Society in Britain, 1750–1914*
    ISBN 0 521 57217 7 (hardback) 0 521 57655 5 (paperback)
34. R. W. Davies, *Soviet Economic Development from Lenin to Khrushchev*
    ISBN 0 521 62260 3 (hardback) 0 521 62742 7 (paperback)
35. H. V. Bowen, *War and British Society, 1688–1815*
    ISBN 0 521 57226 6 (hardback) 0 521 57645 8 (paperback)
36. M. M. Smith, *Debating Slavery: The Antebellum American South*
    ISBN 0 521 57158 8 (hardback) 0 521 57696 2 (paperback)
37. M. Sanderson, *Education and Economic Decline in Britain, 1870 to the 1990s*
    ISBN 0 521 58170 2 (hardback) 0 521 58842 1 (paperback)
38. V. Berridge, *Health Policy, Health and Society, 1939 to the 1990s*
    ISBN 0 521 57230 4 (hardback) 0 521 57641 5 (paperback)
39. M. E. Mate, *Women in Medieval English Society*
    ISBN 0 521 58322 5 (hardback) 0 521 58733 6 (paperback)
40. P. J. Richardson, *Economic Change in China c. 1800–1950*
    ISBN 0 521 58396 9 (hardback) 0 521 63571 3 (paperback)
41. J. E. Archer, *Social Unrest and Popular Protest in England, 1780–1840*
    ISBN 0 521 57216 9 (hardback) 0 521 57656 3 (paperback)
42. K. Morgan, *Slavery, Atlantic Trade and the British Economy, 1660–1800*
    ISBN 0 521 58213 X (hardback) 0 521 58814 6 (paperback)
43. C. W. Chalklin, *The Rise of the English Town, 1650–1850*
    ISBN 0 521 66141 2 (hardback) 0 521 66737 2 (paperback)
44. J. Cohen and G. Federico, *The Growth of the Italian Economy, 1820–1960*
    ISBN 0 521 66150 1 (hardback) 0 521 66692 9 (paperback)
45. T. Balderston, *Economics and Politics in the Weimar Republic*
    ISBN 0 521 58375 6 (hardback) 0 521 77760 7 (paperback)
46. C. Wrigley, *British Trade Unions since 1933*
    ISBN 0 521 57231 2 (hardback) 0 521 57640 7 (paperback)
47. A. Colli, *The History of Family Business, 1850–2000*
    ISBN 0 521 80028 5 (hardback) 0 521 80472 8 (paperback)
48. D. Mühlberger *The Social Bases of Nazism, 1919–1933*
    ISBN 0 521 80285 7 (hardback) 0 521 00372 5 (paperback)

Previously published as

Studies in Economic and Social History

Titles in the series available from the Macmillan Press Limited

Economic History Society

The Economic History Society, which numbers around 3,000 members, publishes the *Economic History Review* four times a year (free to members) and holds an annual conference.

Enquiries about membership should be addressed to

The Assistant Secretary
Economic History Society
PO Box 70
Kingswood
Bristol
BS15 5TB

Full-time students may join at special rates.